# ARENT & PYKE

# ARENT & PYKE

## INTERIORS BEYOND THE PRIMARY PALETTE

JULIETTE ARENT & SARAH~JANE PYKE

# INTRODUCTION

We can still remember the feelings one particular suburban Sydney backyard stirred in us. Standing amid its myriad greens, we were transported to another place, even time. This garden could have been a fictional wonderland or the grounds of an Italian villa, such was its enchanting quality. Part of this magic stemmed from the owners' deep connection to what they had created, and part came from the house's connection to its surrounds. The building and landscape seemed beautifully entwined.

Our response as designers was to enrich those connections, and in a decorative sense the incorporation of green was a natural choice. But the significance of that colour extended beyond the decorative – it became woven through the built-in elements in an evocative layering of hues. The variegated greens of a checkerboard terrazzo floor brought a sense of nostalgia and an other-worldly mood to echo that of the garden. Deep green joinery ensured the very fabric of the house resonated with this tranquil yet vibrant tone. We painted the walls a misty green that blurred the division between interior and exterior, and the treatment of colour in this house became an immersive experience, as alive with feeling as the shifting canvas outside.

For us, to talk about colour is to talk about memory, but also meaning, energy and emotion. To write a book that references colour in its title is to discuss so much more than a choice of floor tile or paint finish for a wall, although these have their place here too. It is part of a larger and deeply nuanced conversation that we have been engaged in for years. And it begins with the concept of joy.

Everything we do is to create visceral joy – that inner thrum of delight where instinct speaks over intellect, heart over head. A beautifully designed space has the power to generate a sense of belonging, comfort and freedom that uplifts your spirit. We believe that power extends even further – a space that fills you with joy can transform how you live.

While it may sound very 'big picture', for us this belief is grounded in rigorous attention to the smallest details. The objects that tell our stories, the colours that call to our senses, the materials that evoke certain moods – all these play a vital part. But even more than that, our focus is on the day-to-day experience of people's lives. We are constantly thinking about the reassuring rituals and intricacies of domestic life – where people make their tea and coffee, where they prepare school lunches, where they place their bags when they get home. We are also deeply interested in the places of connection – where people sit to unwind, to gather, to entertain – and the way people engage with one another in their own space.

Fifteen years ago, when we formed Arent & Pyke, no one was really talking about how design made you *feel*. The focus was on aesthetics and the debates were around trends – old school versus new school, minimalist versus decorative – yet there didn't seem to be enough interest in how a design could impact your life. Or how a house could be lovingly crafted for the unique lifestyle of a family.

From the start, our approach has not been concerned

with trends or generic solutions but rather the dynamic, spirited, colourful and very personal appeal of real-life spaces – the sort of spaces we would like to live in. When we met, we recognised that we shared the same energy and entrepreneurial drive, and the same passion for life – not only the life we wanted to create for ourselves, but the life we wanted to create for our clients. Our intention was to create authentic, meaningful spaces full of verve and vitality that lift the spirit and nurture the soul. It still is, and today we share that vision with our team and our extended network of collaborators.

While 'emotional connection' and 'wellbeing' have become industry buzzwords, we are proud to be leaders in the conversation that now revolves around them. For us, wellbeing and joy are intrinsically linked, and we believe there is much to be learned in terms of the impact great design can have on our lives. We're keenly aware of how much our environment affects our sense of wellbeing, and we want to offer people the best way of living, creating healthy, low-impact homes that help them thrive.

Now, more than ever, that seems essential. Since we started our business, we have witnessed a shift in values to a more inward-looking focus that is literally closer to home – to our local community, our friends and family. Never has the safety and comfort of home been more important, or the need to create joy at home more necessary to strengthen, nurture and replenish us before we look outwards again.

Writing this book has been a chance to reflect on the path of Arent & Pyke – not only how far we have come but also what we want to bring to the future. We are delighted to share our philosophy, our approach and our designs in these pages. For us, the building blocks of a project are not the bricks and mortar but the intangibles that make up our ethos as a business: the transportive and immersive roles of colour, the creation of joy and forging of an emotional connection, the character and spirit of a house – its heart and soul – and that special alchemy that occurs when it all comes together in a unique, magical blend. These ideas are the touchstones of our studio, and the projects we have selected here illustrate how we express those ideas and bring them to life.

We hope that viewing our projects through this lens gives them an extra dimension and prompts a different way of thinking about the spaces we live in. We have never been interested in decoration for decoration's sake – for us, a design should go beyond beauty and function to achieve a timeless, uncontrived quality that ensures a house belongs to those who live in it.

This book explores the rich physical aspects that we know colour can bring to interiors. It ventures into a surprisingly evocative spectrum of soft and subtle shifts in tone but, further than that, it taps into the emotion of design. When a home is brought to life through the colour, character and spirit of its different elements, everything is enriched and all the senses are engaged for a full, joyous living experience.

The experience of joy can be both immediate and far-reaching. It can be as simple as feeling inspired by the colour on a wall and as wonderfully complex as the way a well-designed space can enrich your life.

The projects in this book showcase the results of our rigorous design process. We also wanted to give some insight into the process itself by sharing how we think. Every home and every client bring their own particular requirements so the outcome will always differ, but our approach to each design is guided by the same principles. Five concepts encapsulate our approach and make up our ethos as designers: joy, colour, character, spirit and alchemy. These concepts ensure that our projects have meaning for our clients, forging a strong emotional connection. They are not always tangible but they are always deeply felt and perceived, and they bring a design to life. They are our touchstones and our building blocks.

# THE CONSIDERED CRAFTING OF
# SPACES THAT LIFT THE SPIRIT
# AND NOURISH THE SOUL

1

It sounds simple – we want people to feel happy in their home. But behind this is a deep understanding of the complex psychology of space and the lifestyle and personal journey of each client. We harness all the elements we work with – colour and pattern, material and textile, light and art, line and form – to individually shape each special space.

Home should be a place of nurturing and nourishment. It should be a sanctuary of peace, comfort and security where you feel grounded and free to be yourself. Crafting that place is about fostering an emotional connection and a sense of belonging. Your heart space.

Creating visceral joy is at the heart of all our work. Our focus on how a space feels begins with an appreciation of how people experience living there. Home is the place for recharging and relaxing, and with this in mind we consider both the spaces for interaction and those for reflection. We focus on where people come together, such as the kitchen, living and dining areas. This is where all the action happens and where some of the most joyous moments occur. For us, the kitchen is far more than a functional zone and we strive to make it a warm, vibrant place to congregate, rich with colour, character and tactile pleasure. In the same way, the bedroom is more than somewhere to sleep. It is also a place for repair and recharging, so we design it as a true retreat zone and emotional balm.

Joy and wellbeing are intertwined, and for us a happy home is a healthy home. We want to craft living spaces that soar with feeling and feed the soul. Creating a room that sings with colour sounds simple, yet the emotions it sparks are far from it.

# COLOUR

## THE INFINITE POSSIBILITIES FOR THE EMOTIVE AND THE IMMERSIVE

The meaningful role colour can play in bringing a space to life is a continual source of inspiration for us. We weave colour through the entire fabric of a house at every stage of the design process. Even then, the placement of one last richly hued accessory or artwork can be the element that draws the whole design together. The influence of colour is ongoing and we never stop thinking about it.

We use colour as a device to evoke particular moods and shape the experience of a space, playing with its look in different light to soothe or energise, nurture or revive. We use it to unify spaces, linking new parts of a house to old ones, or crafting a connection between interior and garden. Our approach is not to add a 'pop' of this or 'block' of that – for us, the greatest power of colour lies in its immersive effect, a painterly quality that envelops you so its presence is felt as much as seen. Adding a soft pink tint to the walls of a room can give it a rosy glow that transforms the room – and the feelings it provokes.

Our focus isn't necessarily on the bright and bold colours, although these have their own significant impact. The softer, nuanced tones of the tertiary palette, whose language lies in delicious words like nougat, butter and olive, can unlock the door to a world of emotions. We work a lot with colour combinations, exploring the way different hues interact – room to room, piece to piece – to conjure up an entirely new sensibility. At the heart of it all is our desire to elicit a response, and whether we use colour to create harmony or contrast, it is always with the intention to lift the spirit.

2

# CHARACTER

## THE MEANINGFUL OBJECTS, ARRANGEMENTS AND ELEMENTS THAT TELL THE STORY OF A SPACE

3

The character of a home comes from the elements that reveal its personality and tell its story, from architectural lines and forms to cherished family pieces. Sometimes our design is responding to a story that is already there, such as with heritage buildings. Here, we try to distil the essence of the house's character and meet that in the contemporary language of detail and joinery, subtly referencing the mood of the past while reflecting the client's lifestyle for the future.

At other times we are helping clients to create a new story. Incorporating their own belongings – a favourite artwork, a souvenir from their travels – helps us do this. Not everyone has these to begin with, so during the design process we encourage clients to think about objects in a new way, beyond their decorative or functional role and in a more emotive realm. The story of an interior grows richer, more authentic and more interesting when personal, meaningful elements are woven into it. In this way, the design choices made today can become potent new memories in the future.

One of the most natural and pleasing ways to bring character to a space is through the process of ageing. It might be an old timber table that shows the knocks and cuts acquired over the years, or the faded upholstery of a favourite chair, or a brass doorknob that reveals the frequent attention of human hands. The nicks and patinas are tangible marks of the passage of time and the rituals of life and as such are imbued with meaning. It is one of the reasons we love working with materials like timber, terrazzo and marble – the connection they offer us to nature and its inevitable cycle brings a strong sense of comfort. To us, a home that reflects the beauty of time passing and the ephemeral nature of things is a celebration of life well lived.

# SPIRIT

## THE HEARTBEAT OF A HOME, THE ESSENCE AND DYNAMIC LIFE FORCE OF A SPACE

We want to create homes that are full of spirit and hum with life to reflect the lives of their owners. Much of our work involves imbuing spaces with energy, but that doesn't necessarily mean they have to be lively and vigorous. Different spaces call for different moods, and crafting those moods involves using a range of elements from artworks to the modulation of light. Scale can be a persuasive tool here – we might introduce smaller pieces and more of them, or opt for fewer pieces in a larger scale to make a room feel calmer.

Along with colour, we use pattern to enrich the spirit of a space. We are particularly fond of asymmetric, organic lines that take their cue from the natural world, breathing life into a design, relaxing formal layouts and promoting a sense of ease. And for us, pattern is as much about the inherent details of materials as it is about fabric. An abstract print on a bedhead can lend a playful quality, but the swirls of figured marble, the mix of colours in terrazzo and the pleasing grain of timber also bring their own dynamic and offer the comfort of their tactility. The sensory experience of a home is part of its appeal and we are constantly considering these elements for our clients – how a cushion feels to hold, how a floor feels to walk on. We literally feel our way around each project.

A spirited home is a joyful home, and we believe that central to this is a lighthearted sense of design that exists beyond the practical and purposeful. Home is not the place for the symmetrical and stitched up or the overly formal and tightly wound. We like to incorporate touches of whimsy and optimism purely for their beauty and the happiness they generate. A dreamy wallpaper print, the cheeky form of a chair, an unexpected artwork – these are the moments in a house's life that surprise and delight.

# ALCHEMY

## THE ENCHANTING BLEND OF ELEMENTS AND THE IMPACT OF THE INTANGIBLE

5

Where you drop your bag when you get home, where you make your coffee, sit to read, hang your bathrobe – we delve into and delight in these intricate, important domestic details. We take a deeply empathetic approach in working with our clients, listening to and learning from them, and putting ourselves in their shoes so we can deliver a personal understanding of their lifestyle. The resulting design should feel familiar and intuitive, uniquely crafted to suit the people who live there. Rather like a magician's sleight of hand, it should feel effortless in its experience without revealing all the planning and work behind it.

There is another layer to this magic. We believe there is an alchemy at play in the best of spaces, where all the elements – volume and texture, light and colour, architecture and object – combine to create something truly special that is greater than the sum of its parts. It is a holistic synergy we strive for, considering all these elements together throughout the design process. Added to this are the intangibles – the eliciting of emotions, the building of character, the injection of spirit. The evocative blend of things you can see and things you can feel – this, for us, is the alchemy of joyful design.

SCULPTU

THE

URE SBY

SEA

'AN ECLECTIC MIX
OF PIECES REACHES ACROSS
THE ERAS, EVOKING A SENSE
OF TIMELESSNESS.'

# INTERWEAVING DESIGN STORIES IN
# A MEDITERRANEAN~STYLE HOUSE

**11 colours**

**345 m²**

**3 bedrooms**
**3 bathrooms**
**2 adults**

In the living room, with its views of the sparkling harbour, three gently curved pieces of furniture catch the eye as they capture and reflect the sunlight outside. The first, a cork-topped coffee table with an appealing organic shape, is a mid-century icon by designer Paul T Frankl. The next, a table with a lacquered ash top and pellucid resin legs by Apparatus Studio, is a contemporary piece destined to become a future classic. The third, a drinks cabinet in a glossy burl veneer, is a custom piece we designed in collaboration with an Italian artisan workshop.

Individually, each piece brings its own design story to the space with the rigours of its creative process. Together, this combination of vintage, contemporary and bespoke elements encapsulates our approach to the furnishing of this house. An eclectic mix of pieces reaches across the eras, evoking a sense of timelessness. It's an unusual quality that is present throughout the house, perhaps heightened by its dreamy location, hidden behind a wall of greenery on one side and opening onto the harbour on the other.

When the owners contacted us for this project in Sydney's eastern suburbs, the house had already seen two incarnations in its short life. Built in the early 2000s, it had undergone a sympathetic renovation and redesign about ten years later. Like the previous residents, these new owners loved much about the house, particularly its Mediterranean feel and exterior stonework, but they wanted to update the interiors to reflect their own style.

Respect for a house's legacy is at the heart of our approach, even when the house is relatively young. A new interior design needn't mean ripping everything out and starting again, so, where possible, we embrace the chance to build upon the strengths we see. With these clients, we wanted to make a sensitive response to the existing interior architecture of this house. There were several elements that we were eager to retain, such as architect Daniel Boddam's sculptural staircase with its stucco finish, the polished plaster walls in their shade of parchment, and designer Cameron Kimber's fabric-panelled bedroom walls in rich crimson hues. For us, this design process was not about removal and destruction, but enhancement and evolution.

A luminous example is the master ensuite, which featured walls in grey marble and a floor made from teak boat decking. To bring more light into the room, we added another layer of stone to the walls – a cream-coloured marble with delicate veins that span a warm spectrum from gold through to rust. The combination of the two layers enriches the tonality and mood of the space, brightening it and bringing a cosy glow that is intensified

by a pink Venetian glass wall sconce. The only other changes we made were to add a mirrored panel to one wall and new vanities to complement the new finishes, while retaining the freestanding bath and tapware.

In the master bedroom, the walls were again our starting point. These were covered in an Indian sari fabric of red block-print flowers, which together with the matching curtains created a lovely sense of being enveloped in colour and pattern. To make the room a little less formal, we broke up the expanse of pattern by changing the curtains on either side of the bed to soft white linen and placing matchstick blinds behind them. The shift in materials lightens and relaxes the space, and we continued this by incorporating different textural elements – a custom woven sisal bedhead, a vintage cane daybed, vintage timber bedside tables and an iconic Akari paper lamp by Isamu Noguchi.

Our designs often involve softening and relaxing formal spaces. A mix of contrasting textures serves the same purpose in the living room, where the cork, resin and burl veneer pieces sit alongside vintage cane chairs, bouclé and leather sofas, a sisal rug and a colourful vintage rug. We added the vintage rug to make the room more dynamic, and the furniture layout can be altered to suit the occasion. The flowing shape of the custom bouclé sofa, which takes its cue from the curved staircase, allows it to relate to the fireplace but also to the rest of the room and the view outside.

On the other side of the stairs, a different custom piece plays a similar role. In marble the colour of sea foam, the kitchen island forms a generous organic shape at one end, creating a convivial seating area that invites you to look out at the water. Beneath the smooth honed slab of the benchtop, we carved a series of fine V-shaped grooves that soften the look of the island's base. Viewing the island from afar, you observe the subtle movement of greens rather than the piece of stone itself, an effect that is enhanced by other tones we introduced into the space, such as the olive green of the Venetian glass chandelier and the golden olive of the cabinetry.

Those handmade and bespoke elements are responses to the artisanal quality of the interior architecture. Details like the hand-stitched linen curtains in the sitting room and the paisley fabric panelling in the rumpus room honour the building. At the foot of the stairs sit a custom dining table and console, designed so one can fit into the other when extra space is required. Made from contrasting timbers, they are individually beautiful pieces, yet their curves merge to create a wonderful whole, just like the layers of the house itself.

The sitting room is the first place you see on entering the house, and we wanted to create a sense of arrival with an inviting space that doesn't take itself too seriously. An appealing mix of elements – and a touch of the unexpected – lies at the centre of this. The timber and rattan chairs, discovered at the Clignancourt flea markets in Paris, are among the many vintage pieces in the house chosen for the beauty they bring to a space rather than their connection to a particular decade. The wave motif of the curtains that frame the harbour views beyond introduces a surprising and gently witty detail that lifts the whole room.

A SENSE OF ARRIVAL

**ABOVE**
One of the many beautiful vintage pieces in the house, the 1960s Murano glass chandelier
was introduced to elevate the kitchen beyond the functional. Placing a piece this notable above
the unusually shaped end of the marble island marks this as a special place to perch.

**OPPOSITE**
Against the new paisley fabric-lined walls of the rumpus room, a painting
by McLean Edwards offers a compelling focal point.

TREE

'THE INTERIOR DESIGN CALLED FOR AN ALCHEMY OF NATURAL ELEMENTS, COLOUR, TEXTURE, LIGHTING AND ARTWORKS.'

# NATURE AND CULTURE MEET IN A FEDERATION WORKER'S COTTAGE

**7 colours**

**180 m²**

**3 bedrooms**
**2 bathrooms**
**2 adults**
**2 children**

The giant fiddle-leaf fig growing through the centre of this house in Sydney's inner west was always going to influence our design approach. But it also revealed a great deal about the owners. The fact that they allowed so much space for an internal tree in a building with an extremely small footprint, rather than opt for extra storage or more furniture, told us this was a family for whom living in their house was as much about the experience as it was about the objects. Bringing them more such experiences through the interior design called for an alchemy of natural elements, colour, texture, lighting and artworks.

This tiny Federation worker's cottage had already undergone an incredible renovation at the hands of architects Welsh + Major when we joined the project. Their ingenious vision had transformed it from a skinny single-storey structure to a two-storey home that appears vast in scale and length. New volumes extend vertically through the void around the tree and horizontally through the extension, which opens onto a courtyard designed by landscape architect Sue Barnsley. Every inch of space seems dedicated to maximising the available light and outdoor connection, and the tree and the retractable roof above offer the strongest connection of all.

For the owners, Natalie and Keiron, the tree was a nostalgic reference to South Africa, where the palaver tree is traditionally a community meeting place for discussions, ideas and storytelling. The lightwell in which this fig sits is positioned between the old and new parts of the house, enhancing the feeling of spaciousness and illuminating the usually dark centre of the terrace layout.

Our first step was to introduce other sources of light. We used wall sconces, floor lamps and pendants to encapsulate the essence of spaces. Perhaps the most pivotal addition is the orb-like Akari lantern that hangs over the dining table, creating a gentle ambient glow in the deepest part of the house with the lowest ceiling. From there, our furnishing concept for the dining area evolved as we replaced an existing white contemporary table with a shapely timber one and added dining chairs upholstered in olive velvet.

Seemingly simple choices were a considered response to the materiality of the house. The bagged brickwork and exposed sandstone on the walls, the concrete stairs and floor, and the black-stained original timber are robust elements that in another space could be viewed as industrial. However, we saw a raw, grounded quality in them, and a single slab of forest green marble at the base of the stairs also revealed a level of refinement. We set out

to enhance that grounded feel, tempering any sharpness with a natural palette and materials. In the dining area, the texture of timber, the glowing light and the colour of the chairs provide a comforting earthiness, while the sumptuous velvet brings another layer of softness and sophistication.

The spatial manipulation Welsh + Major achieved led to our own exercise in reduction and a balancing act where, with fewer pieces in a shared space, each piece must work harder without overshadowing the next. The long leather sofa in mossy green is the hero of the living area, yet it doesn't steal the limelight from the dining setting. The vintage Ushak rug beneath it is similar in tonality to the floor, creating a seamlessness that suits the space, and a custom ottoman is tucked underneath a small travertine coffee table. Under suspended shelving opposite, a built-in sofa we created from a bench seat offers a calm retreat and a mid-century chaise lends its slender lines to the small transition space at the foot of the stairs. Each piece is appropriate to its space and the different elements sing to each other, creating a strong synergy.

Some of the most vocal elements are the artworks – all heartfelt choices for these clients. We had pictured a wall of several different works behind the sofa, but when the furnishings were in place it was clear one large piece would be more appropriate. Despite its size, Judith Wright's subtle, enigmatic abstract emits a dreamy mood with its palette of inky blues and almost translucent white. It completes the room, playing up to the scale rather than breaking it down as it reaches for the high ceiling.

In the upstairs extension, Leah Fraser's painting brings a romantic layer and dynamic element to the master bedroom. To introduce more softness to the small room with its bagged brick walls, we added linen curtains in off-white with a band of mustard that aligns with the base of the window. Here, we created a little ledge for displaying objects, to give the room a more personal feeling. An armchair and vintage Moroccan rug calm it further, while the bedding, with its strong chartreuse throw layered over a pink linen bedhead, is a response to the artwork and a continuation of the house's earthy tones.

The final artwork we introduced was a contemporary photograph by Christian Thompson AO. The native flora, colours and materials in his self-portrait work beautifully in the dining area, and the couple's two children also enjoy the feeling that an extra guest joins them for dinner every night. This is the particular allure of art and furnishings that we cherish. It encourages people to interact with their surroundings, enticing them to smile, talk, exchange ideas and create new stories under their own family tree.

In a house where scale is so important, both the sofa settings illustrate the persuasive power of 'less is more'. Furnishing a small space with a lot of petite pieces will only make it appear smaller – and busier. Using fewer pieces – one long sofa and one sizeable rug – creates a sense of visual calm. The built-in sofa maximises the width of this room and sits low to the ground, allowing the suspended timber and brass shelving to draw the eye upwards and emphasise the vertical volume of the space.

# ENHANCING VOLUME

ABOVE
A selection of lovingly curated handmade and vintage ceramics adds to the earthy,
textural elements in the house.

THE

OF

COPATH

PATH

COLOUR

'COLOUR LEADS YOU
THROUGH THIS HOUSE
AND PROVIDES ITS
MEMORABLE MOMENTS.'

# HARMONISING PALETTE AND PROPORTION IN A GRAND SANDSTONE HOUSE

9 colours

335 m²

5 bedrooms
3 bathrooms
2 adults
3 children

It was the last piece we introduced to the design of this historic house, yet it perfectly encapsulates the owners' lifestyle. Situated in the courtyard of this 1885 sandstone building on Sydney's north shore, the custom-poured terrazzo table is ideal for feasting. Its generous scale and weight give it a gravitas that suits the large space, announcing it as a special place to congregate. The varied flecks of green draw in all the hues of the vast surrounding gardens, connecting the house to its natural setting.

The owners never planned to move until they set eyes on this majestic house with its wraparound verandahs and manicured gardens across 1500 square metres of land. Charmed by its heritage, Virginia and Andrew sought our help to refresh the interiors in a way that respected the elegance of the building but was still relaxed and livable for them and their three young children. Due to their large family network, entertaining is a major part of their lives, and a lovely sense of readiness for any gathering pervades the design, particularly on the lower floor.

The grand proportions of the two front rooms allowed us to play with scale in two very different ways that reflect the purpose of each space. In the formal living room, we wanted to balance traditional elements with the fresh contemporary sensibility of the artworks, palette and furnishings. Long linen curtains pooling gently on the floor celebrate the height of the room with a lightness that counteracts its formality. Their ecru tone works beautifully with the original timber frames. Nothing here is white. Instead, the room features soft colours and pleasing forms and textures – a curvaceous pink sofa and cream bouclé armchairs, caramel cork coffee tables, an ivory rug and walls, and a ceiling painted the palest green.

With French doors at either end, the living room connects the front garden to the courtyard. At the rear of the room, a more formal mood is created by a piano and a bar fashioned from heritage-listed bookshelves. We added grey mirror behind the shelves, which we created from marble slabs of different colours. The lowest shelf, in the rich burgundy tone of Rosso Levanto marble, extends to form an integrated tabletop that sits on a brass base. With two stools, and forest green cupboards beneath, it is an elegant entertainment space.

Across the hall, the children's playroom features the same pooling curtains and is just as grand in scale, but with different diversions in mind. We wanted to make it a dynamic room by playing to its height while bringing more volume and interest into the middle space. The black-and-white wallpaper features oversized animal outlines dotted with colour, while a large storage cupboard presents a fun, attractive form in shades from garnet through marmalade to sky blue. With more hues in the rug, artwork and soft green sofa and chair, the space is lively yet still stylish.

Throughout the house, there is an interplay between spaces for family and spaces for visitors, where the beauty of colour and materiality are for the enjoyment of all. This is particularly evident in the powder room beneath the stairs – a space made more special by the intricacy of its details. The basin sits in an eye-catching alcove of Verde Esmeralda marble, featuring glazed green tiles behind brass tapware and a rattan-framed mirror. The marble's dreamy green continues in a petite wall-mounted shelf and a lip that runs around the wall, separating the stucco finish above from the beaded American oak panels below. Despite the room's position, it emanates a welcoming glow due to the honeyed tones of the timber and the pale grey and white marble of the mosaic floor.

The two upstairs bathrooms are just as appealing, evoking a sense of serenity that suits the retreat areas on this floor. Travertine brings warmth to the main bathroom in the custom fluted bath, skirting, splashback and vanity top, and timber cabinets feature more bead detail. The earthy tones are complemented by grey Moroccan terracotta tiles in the shower recess, and blue concrete floor tiles in a bow tie pattern add a vibrant flourish.

The master ensuite is a symphony of soft pinks, with a shower enclosure of tiles so lusciously glazed they look as if they have been iced. The tones deepen with the purple swirls of Calacatta Viola marble, which we used for the top of the timber vanity, the mirror frames and skirting. To complete the delicate details of this feminine space, we had the marble cut down to create mosaic floor tiles.

In a quiet palette shift, pale blue curtains bring a tranquil vibe to the master bedroom, offset by the warmth and texture of the golden rug, timber floors and the grasscloth inlay on timber-framed wardrobe doors that span the length of the room.

Colour leads you through this house and provides its memorable moments. Down the stairs, with their custom green runner, green hues return you to the gathering areas – the casual living room with its sea green rug and grass-toned sofa, where the family spend so much of their time, and the outdoor spaces with that welcoming terrazzo table. The power of this monumental piece links the inside and outside of this home and brings people together.

We like to think of powder rooms as little jewel boxes – these compact spaces can make a big impression, lending themselves to a more spirited and unique design. This might mean using flamboyant wallpaper, strong finishes or intriguing colour choices. In this special room under the stairs, the richness and variety of materials bring the magic. The contrast of the stucco wall, the Verde Esmeralda marble, the glossy green tiles and the timber panels with their ribbing detail creates an intensity of layers that surprises and delights.

# SMALL AND SPECIAL

ABOVE
There is an almost monastic sense of calm in the main bathroom, created by the soft texture
of the stucco walls and the earthy nature of the fluted travertine bath and travertine skirting
across the blue concrete tiles.

OPPOSITE
The serene pairing of materiality and palette continues in the master bedroom. The grasscloth
inlay of the wardrobe, the woollen rug and the straw S-Chair by Tom Dixon for Cappellini
bring their own textural interplay amid the cool blue tones.

FRAME

FOR

'THE SPIRIT OF THE HOUSE CELEBRATES THE ARTISTRY OF COLOUR AND TEXTURE IN DEFINING A MOOD.'

# COLOURFUL FAMILY SPACES
# IN A FEDERATION BUNGALOW

**10 colours**

**280 m²**

**4 bedrooms**
**3 bathrooms**
**2 adults**
**3 children**

Spaces for nurture and nourishment. Spaces for relaxing and recharging. Spaces for congregating, or just contemplating. We think about all these things when approaching an interior design, looking at how people live in their house as we consider ways to enhance their living experience. It might be as complex and nuanced as the emotions evoked by the colour of a room, or as simple as the tactile pleasure elicited by running a hand along a textured wall.

For the owners, Jacqueline and Dylan, and their three children, the renovation of their four-bedroom Federation bungalow in Sydney's inner west centred around creating a robust, comfortable series of spaces that could accommodate extended family gatherings. Cooking and entertaining are cherished priorities here, so we knew that the open-plan kitchen and dining area, part of the new two-storey addition to the house, was going to be a focus of the design.

We also knew that this would be an area where kids love to congregate. One of our first steps was the introduction of a timber-lined window nook with a cushioned bench seat, which faces the kitchen and frames a view of the pool outside. Snack area, homework space and chill-out zone, it presents a beautiful moment of stillness in the rhythm of the house, and is painted a serene forest green that is soft and inviting. It is also central to the spirit of the house, celebrating the artistry of colour and texture in defining a mood, and showcasing how intimate areas can be created within large architectural volumes.

The nook sits beside a double-height void that was designed as part of the extension by architects Carter Williamson. Flooded with sunshine, the void highlights the kitchen and dining area as heart and hub, but its generous scale had to be tempered to ensure the proportions related to family life. This is where materiality wields such a transformative power. The texture that can be created with materials such as timber and stone brings surfaces into focus, reducing the scale of the space from the architectural to the personal.

Having laid oak floorboards in a herringbone pattern, which brought lovely detail to the room, we worked with the architects to also line the ceiling and trim the void with oak. The timber panels make the ceiling a feature, visually drawing it closer while also providing a softer look against the room's black steel window frames. In contrast to the natural finish of the floors and timber dining table, we added a lime wash to the ceiling. This not only brings out the grain of the wood but also gives it a luminous, reflective quality that enlivens the whole area. An aptly named Floatation pendant light by Ingo Maurer completes the effect, bridging the gap further by hovering gracefully above the dining table.

Materiality transforms other areas, such as the staircase, where we introduced a ribbed detail to the rendering on the stair wall, together with a banded rail and matching capping in dark stained timber. In a large space that could have consisted purely of smooth white planes, this mix of textures delivers sculptural elements that can be touched and enjoyed. Around the fireplace in the new living room, we added glazed bricks and a roughly rendered wall for the tactility they bring.

There is something else at play here too – the intertwined language of old and new, which is fundamental to our work. With so many projects involving extensions to original houses, we are constantly looking for ways to connect the two spaces. For us, it comes down to a respect for both – responding to one while embracing the other. In this house, new elements like the exposed brickwork and rough rendering hark back to the solid, earthy character of the original building. In the same way, the new timber ceiling in the kitchen nods to the ornate treatment of ceilings in the older rooms.

Colour also has much to say in this dialogue between old and new. Joyous hues beckon from different rooms in the original part of the house. The rich yellow walls of the front sitting room create a sunburst effect which, when teamed with pink linen curtains, gives the place a gorgeous glow. The colours work with the informal furniture and vibrant vintage rug to energise the space, making a traditionally formal room more casual and appealing.

The muted blue walls of the study evoke a quieter mood, while the lilac walls and saffron rug in the girls' bedroom are a delectable combination. Colour acts as a guide, leading from these rooms into the extension. The doors and reveals along the original hallway are painted coral pink – a hue that connects to the peach tones in the terrazzo slabs of the kitchen benchtops and splashback. Here, the pink is paired with grey and white marble, which forms an elegant wall above the splashback and a surprisingly delicate layer beneath the island benchtop. With cabinetry in mushroom tones, the room speaks of warmth and welcome.

Neutral tones soften the new areas, such as the shell-pink walls of the master bedroom and ensuite and the nougat walls of the living room, but playful bold splashes also appear in a bright lemon-print bedhead fabric, rust-red dining chairs and a burnt-orange armchair. Like the timber nook and the painted walls, each colour enhances the living experience for this family, offering spaces for rest, spaces for play and all the spaces in-between that make up a life.

ABOVE
With its lining of timber painted forest green, the window nook is a calming place to
congregate. The custom bench seat is grouped with woven Artek chairs, a vintage travertine
table and a vintage light.

OPPOSITE
In the adjacent dining area, a dk3 Tree table is surrounded by Wishbone chairs by Carl Hansen
& Søn in russet – a classic with a twist. The architectural volume creates an abundance of light
that brings the texture of the materiality into focus.

A FRAME FOR LIVING

The palette of this children's bedroom has an impact that can almost be felt, due to the treatment of what is essentially a duality of tones. The luscious sweep of lilac walls in Dulux Artist's Shadow and the warm expanse of saffron in the custom silk rug by Tappeti have a wonderfully immersive effect. Reducing the decorative scheme to this rather unexpected pairing also heightens the sense of drama in the room. Against that dreamy setting, custom bedheads upholstered in Vases, a fabric we commissioned from Sydney-based textile company EDIT, provide a sprinkling of pretty detail.

IMMERSIVE COLOUR

DY

BLUE

'THESE BLUES, ENTRANCING WITHOUT BEING OVERPOWERING, BRING A JOY TO THESE SPACES THAT MAKES THEM AS SPECIAL AS OLD FRIENDS.'

# TWO HUES THAT SING
# IN AN 1880S TERRACE

**8 colours**

**350 m²**

**5 bedrooms**
**3 bathrooms**
**2 adults**
**2 dogs**

Vipere and Kolya. They could be characters from a novel, but they are in fact the names of paint colours – two incredibly evocative shades of blue that we used on the walls of this 1880s terrace. We know them well, because we have been asked about them often since the finished house was featured in the media. One of the things we love about working with colour is how strongly it resonates with people.

This was one of our first forays into the immersive approach to colour that we now embrace. We undertook the design and decorative work for this three-storey house in Sydney's eastern suburbs in the early days of our business. A lengthy three-year process, it proved a turning point in our evolution as designers, both in terms of how we use colour and how we approach the interiors of heritage houses.

Steve and James had owned the terrace for several years and, after living in New York for much of that time, they were ready to bring it back to its former glory and make it their own. This is a journey we enjoy, where all involved are keen to stay sympathetic to the era of the house, maintaining its character while adapting it for a modern lifestyle. The aim was to respect the grandeur of the house's proportions but make it more intimate and personal, even a little playful, while giving a fresh sense of purpose and joy to the rooms.

There are limitations to what you can do with heritage houses, but these often challenge us to create the most interesting moments. Part of our work with architect Tom Ferguson involved repurposing upstairs rooms, which allowed us to create a magical zone incorporating the master bedroom, walk-in robe and ensuite. The latter two spaces used to be another bedroom, and the robe acts as a dividing wall. What unites the spaces and creates a cocooning feeling is the Fornasetti cloud wallpaper with its whimsical, gossamer-light linework in grey and white. In the ensuite, we created an elevated platform for the bath to facilitate draining while retaining the floorboards. Surrounded by Carrara marble (a classic stone that suits the house's restrained elegance) and topped with grey terrazzo, this platform offers a special sanctuary in the sophisticated black-and-white space.

We applied a Black Japan stain to the kauri pine floors upstairs as a way of connecting the robe and ensuite to the master bedroom. Our focus was on taming the proportions of the huge room, which we approached by almost over-sizing the furnishings. Two pendant lights address the symmetrical architecture, and a vast rug and a freestanding wardrobe that is more than two metres tall break down the scale even more. We extended the dimensions of the bed by adding a bench seat at its foot and a series of framed black-and-white maps of Paris on the wall behind it.

A Knoll Saarinen Womb chair already owned by the couple introduced an intensity of colour that sparked many of our palette choices. The room doesn't receive much natural light in the day, so we introduced the warmth by using colour. The toasty mustard hue of the velvet bench seat works with the red tone of the chair. The ivory linen curtains feature a decadent silk banding at their base that looks as if it has been dipped in butterscotch. Against these, the gloriously moody, inky blue of Vipere on the walls creates an intimate, deeply nurturing space.

Downstairs, Kolya makes its mark. This is a lighter, more classic Wedgwood shade of blue that enriches the living and dining areas. We wanted to transform these adjoining formal spaces to make spending time there an everyday occasion, not just a special one. Rather than having an unused dining room full of empty chairs, we set up the space as a library. An antique extendable table at the centre can easily be used for entertaining by adding matching chairs that are otherwise happily scattered around the house.

In the sitting room, the layout may still be formal but the pieces are more relaxed. Taking our cue from the Womb chair upstairs, we introduced some mid-century designs, like a pair of Gerrit Rietveld Utrecht chairs in playfully mismatched blues. These are joined in spirit by the sofa opposite, which features a bold leaf print that is fun, rather than fusty, due to the sofa's contemporary shape. Tying everything together are ivory linen curtains, this time with vertical bandings in navy silk that visually pull ceiling and floor closer for a cosier feel.

Those two beautiful blues owe their existence to another colour in the house. The crisp, pared-back kitchen that we designed for the owners was always going to feature their Enzo Mari screenprint of a bright red apple. The print needed another vivid colour to balance it, and so the idea for an emerald green kitchen cabinet was born. From here, our talk turned to all the jewel tones in the house, and suddenly the neutral walls we had been considering seemed a bit staid.

The clients' willingness to try new tones and their faith in us inspired us to make these bolder choices – choices that now come more naturally. These blues, entrancing without being overpowering, bring a joy to these spaces that makes them as special as old friends.

The iconic Knoll Saarinen Womb chair, upholstered in red woollen bouclé, inspired our palette choices for the master bedroom. We used the deep, stormy blue of Dulux Vipere on the walls to make the room feel more intimate and cocooning, while the addition of yellow in the furnishings brings warmth and completes a trio that references a mid-century palette. Golden tones appear in the mustard mohair velvet upholstery on the custom bench seat and the butterscotch silk from Zimmer + Rohde on the curtains.

# THE CASE FOR PRIMARIES

BROAD SP

ECTRUM

'THIS IS A HOUSE WHERE THE LANGUAGE OF DETAIL AND TEXTURE CONTINUES BETWEEN ROOMS.'

# THE EXPERIENCE OF COLOUR IN A FORMER WORKER'S COTTAGE

**14 colours**

**370 m²**

**4 bedrooms**
**5 bathrooms**
**2 adults**
**3 children**
**2 dogs**

Sometimes the application of colour is so immersive that it becomes more of a felt sensation than a visual effect. You don't necessarily pause to observe the colour, it becomes part of your experience of an interior. At other times, of course, colour provides a vibrant layer that fills your vision with its intensity. In this newly renovated house in Sydney's eastern suburbs, it takes on both captivating roles.

After several years living in New York and Hong Kong, the owners, Betty and Richard, had returned to Sydney with their three children and were ready to resume family life in a place that felt uniquely theirs. The former worker's cottage had been gutted and redeveloped into a larger house by architect Sam Crawford, and we were engaged to bring our particular approach to colour, materiality and furnishing to get the most out of each space.

Working with some of the couple's furniture and artworks, we set about enriching the palette of the adjoining dining and living areas, which we opened up by removing a block of timber joinery that was separating them. Around the existing dining table, classic mid-century chairs upholstered in a rust-toned wool melange present a warm, welcoming setting. A deep green rug adds another dimension to the room's palette, and a richly hued abstract painting brings a burst of colour and energy.

This dynamic quality continues in the living area, with the bold hues of another artwork and a colourful patterned Nepalese rug. These are balanced by more neutral tones in the owners' sofa, a new custom curved sofa in ivory bouclé and a pair of textural cane armchairs. There was already a fireplace in this room, but we relocated it to the centre of the wall to create a more formal layout and installed bookshelves on either side. The oak joinery is painted a creamy pink nougat shade that takes on more meaning as it appears throughout the house. At the base of the shelves, we created little bench seats in the same travertine as the fireplace. The bench seat is a feature we love to incorporate – it delivers a perspective that is often disregarded yet can be the most satisfying, as it faces all the room's vitality.

Both living and dining areas look onto the new kitchen, which is a glorious explosion of colour and materiality. Floor-to-ceiling cabinetry in glossy hand-painted bottle green blends tonally with the stunning green swirls of Verde Guatemala marble, which covers the island and back benchtops and extends up along the joinery reveals. Oak shelving inside the joinery and glazed off-white Moroccan tiles on the splashback and rangehood bring more beautiful finishes, while a burl veneer lends richness and warmth to the island base. At one end of the island, two green marble pillars support a bar area and perching spot, and two iconic adjustable pendant lights can be pulled down to create a pool of light that glows on the green marble.

These elements enhance the island's appeal as a unique piece of furniture in a kitchen that feels opulent yet not overly formal. It is special enough for entertaining, without being too refined for everyday life. We came to understand the importance of this for our clients – after living in different houses, they required spaces with a big individual impact for them to be able to claim this place as their own.

Working with the burl to balance all that green are the peach terrazzo floors we introduced in the kitchen. We believe pink is the perfect foil for green, and that palette interplay also occurs in the master suite upstairs. Betty also encouraged us to embrace colour and pattern in the bedrooms, and the fabric choices on the bedheads reflect this. In the master bedroom, the dark green velvet bedhead by colour aficionado India Mahdavi, with its pink and ivory pattern, sets the tone for a sumptuous space. The bedhead is teamed with burl bedside tables and a carpet in deep coral pink. In the adjacent walk-in robe, a softer green appears in the eucalyptus-coloured joinery, offset by the coral-hued carpet.

Unifying both spaces and connecting them to the ensuite is the pinkish nougat colour of the downstairs bookshelves, which washes over the walls and ceilings of these rooms. It softens the interiors, enveloping you without shouting its presence, and adds character and comfort while complementing the house's contemporary aesthetic. In the ensuite, a room that was formerly all white, the colour also anchors the strong blend of materials – the burl veneer of the vanity cupboards, and the pinky purple vein of Calacatta Viola marble on the vanity benchtop and in the architraves of the entry, shower and toilet recesses.

This is a house where the language of detail and texture continues between rooms. The marble architraves feature a double bullnose element that we used in the travertine fireplace downstairs, and the curved edge of the kitchen island reveals a similar consideration of detail. Kitchen and ensuite share the same Moroccan wall tiles and peach terrazzo floors, while that nougat hue reappears just off the kitchen, on the walls and ceilings of both the walk-in pantry and cellar. It enhances the experience of those smaller areas and is a reminder that the power of colour exists as much in the quieter moments as the bold statements, defining the different spaces that turn a house into a home.

For us, marble not only brings colour, texture and movement but also the rich legacy of its history and its own natural beauty, which changes over time. In this deeply layered kitchen, Verde Guatemala marble adds its intense green to a strong scheme, delivering a pleasing tactility in a space that is all about touch. It is one of the three different types of marble we used in the house and sits beautifully alongside the purples and pinks of Calacatta Viola in the master ensuite and the creamy greens and greys of Arabescato Vagli in the powder room. Each stone brings the remarkable individuality of its colours and markings to the spaces.

THE DRAMA
OF MARBLE

With its persuasive sense of movement, the painting by Ildiko Kovacs energises both the dining
and adjacent living spaces, drawing warmth from the rust tones of Knoll Saarinen Executive
chairs. In rich contrast are the glossy blue lacquered finish of a Cassina Bramante cabinet and
the deep green rug by Robyn Cosgrove.

OPPOSITE
Amid the sumptuously layered palette of the kitchen, two classic white Flos Diabolo pendant
lights by Achille Castiglioni provide a crisp, refreshing accent.

The luxury of proportion and the softness of light and colour transform the master ensuite into a dreamy, nurturing space. The walls and ceiling are painted in the same nougat tones of Dulux Bongo Drum that appear in other parts of the house, and harmonise beautifully with the milky hand-glazed Moroccan wall tiles, the Calacatta Viola marble and burl of the vanity, and the peach terrazzo floors. Floating curtains gently distil the light, enhancing the gracious quality of this elegant room.

# SEA

CHANGE

'TIMELESS DESIGN CAN
BE LIGHTHEARTED AS
WELL AS BEAUTIFUL.'

# TRANSFORMING SPACES IN A BEACHSIDE HOUSE

7 colours

280 m²

4 bedrooms
4 bathrooms
2 adults
2 children

We often talk about clients coming on a journey with us during the design process, but that can go both ways, particularly when the process takes several years. Just as a client joins us in embracing new ideas for their house, we adapt our vision to meet their changing lifestyle. The design of this house evolved through time, as our client's life shifted from that of a busy bachelor to a married man with a baby on the way.

Sanil was drawn to the quiet beachside location of his house, with its surrounding bushland and lofty ocean views. Designed by architect David Boyle and with a landscaped native garden by Pangkarra Garden Design, the building evokes a 1950s Australian coastal vernacular through elements like a raked ceiling of hoop-pine panels and expansive timber floors. When we were first engaged to furnish the house, our interior design was a response to the way the architecture sat in the landscape and maintained a connection from outdoors to indoors. Six years and a wedding later, Sanil and his wife, Karyn, sought our help to create a home that would address the needs of their growing family and set them up for the future.

Reviewing the design through a new lens saw some spaces barely change and others transform, but the one constant was the owners' developing appreciation for handmade and well-crafted furniture and artworks.

With its ocean views and timber ceiling, the main living area upstairs was designed in neutral tones and natural, easy-weathering materials. It has a relaxed look that displays an elegance of line in pieces like a pair of iconic leather chairs. A travertine block along one wall began our own romance with that material, which continued throughout the house over the years. The stone's soft, sandy appearance gives it an appealing earthiness that suits the mix of textures in this space.

The adjacent dining setting is a composition of strong, striking gestures. A solid timber table made from two planks of oak is surrounded by the graphic black lines of the dining chairs, the long-stemmed light and the charcoal and pencil artworks on the wall. Beside it, a woven timber cabinet by Caroline Casey and a paper sculpture commissioned from Anna-Wili Highfield are significant pieces that emerged from an ongoing discussion with Sanil about Australian design and art.

With a new baby sleeping downstairs, our attention turned to a second living area on this floor where the family was spending more time. While upstairs living was all about the view, this room looked out onto the garden and landscaped area. Its location and lower ceilings gave it a more inward-facing aspect and we wanted to create a cosier ambience, layering the space with the colours and patterns that both owners love. A vibrant vintage rug on the concrete floor went a long way towards achieving this, bringing richness and character to the room. So too does the warm milky shade we used to paint the walls and ceilings, which gives everything an incandescent glow.

We replaced a wall of simple timber joinery with a fireplace flanked by cabinets painted soft green beneath a top of rich green marble. The combination anchors the room, giving it a more robust feeling. On another wall, a Mitch Cairns artwork adds its scattering of green leaves to a lively mix of pieces that includes a vividly upholstered cane chair and oak side tables resembling wooden crates.

Upstairs, the couple's passion for craft is reflected in the timberwork of the kitchen island that features vertically slatted timber doors, through which the horizontal drawers can be seen, creating an intricate interplay of layers and lines. At one end we created a breakfast bar with leather tiles, which are wonderfully tactile, surprisingly hard-wearing and will age beautifully over time.

Colour and pattern form a serene space in the master bedroom, where a bedhead of blue paisley fabric pairs beautifully with the grey-green walls. The delicacy of an Akari paper light sculpture is offset by the textured finishes of the sisal floor and a travertine block that acts as a bedside table. Testament to its appeal for these owners, the room has hardly changed over the years, and the paisley is so pleasing we gave a nod to it in the warm tones of the bedhead in another bedroom downstairs.

We welcomed the chance to introduce more earthy travertine in the bathrooms, where the focus is on materiality and form, enhanced by a few joyful design follies. In the master ensuite, a wall-mounted travertine basin makes an attractive partner to a shelf topped in heavenly peach-coloured terrazzo, which also covers the floor and main vanity top. The hand of different designers can be seen in the unique lines of an Eileen Gray mirror and in the timberwork of a Carl Hansen & Søn cupboard and Artek screen.

Another wall-mounted travertine basin forms the centrepiece of the downstairs powder room, beside a cloud-shaped shelf of peachy terrazzo. The unusual combination of a custom mirror and rattan wall light ensures that the elements in this room will continue to charm for years. It is delightful proof that timeless design can be lighthearted as well as beautiful.

Time has seen all the spaces of this house touched in some way. The design has moved both house and owners into a new era and, with a second baby now on the scene, more elements may change and others will remain, but all will be part of that same rewarding journey.

**ABOVE**
Against the warm planes of timber on the floors, ceiling and dk3 Tree table,
the black graphic lines of the Thonet Le Corbusier chairs offer striking contrast.
These are joined to dramatic effect by the long wall light and artworks by John Reid (left)
and Nyapanyapa Yunupingu (right), one of a pair in this space.

**OPPOSITE**
A woven timber cabinet by Caroline Casey hosts a thoughtful melding of different artistic
disciplines that includes a vase by Alana Wilson and a sculpture by Anna-Wili Highfield beside
the second artwork by Nyapanyapa Yunupingu. This ensemble creates a beautiful entry moment
at the top of the stairs that is made more significant by the owners' passion for collecting works
by local artists.

ABOVE

Colour, texture and form contribute to the character of the master ensuite. The timber Artek screen presents an attractive fluid shape and echoes the warm tones of the peach terrazzo floor, while the rotund legs of the Water Monopoly bath give it a charming persona all its own.

OPPOSITE

In the master bedroom, the Akari 10A floor lamp by Isamu Noguchi casts its ethereal glow on walls painted in Dulux Hildegard and the bedhead, upholstered in Jamawar fabric by Penny Morrison.

The dynamic nature of this powder room stems in part from the pleasing tension created by the different shapes and textures. Sharp angles contrast with strong curves, the handwoven wall light offsets other smooth finishes, and the shine of the mirror gleams against the matte of the wall. The applied finish of micro-cement, tinted to match the walls throughout the house, gives this wall a soft appearance. This in turn contrasts with the harder surfaces of stone in the travertine basin and terrazzo shelf, adding another level of interest to a playful design.

PLAYING
WITH CONTRASTS

'LUXURY IS FOUND IN
A GENEROSITY OF SPACE,
A SENSE OF SERENITY AND
A RICHNESS OF COLOUR
AND MATERIALS.'

# RESTORING THE HEART
# IN A 1920S APARTMENT

7 colours

220 m²

3 bedrooms
2 bathrooms
2 adults

In many ways, this is a love story. It certainly was for us. When we first saw this pretty 1928 apartment in Sydney's eastern suburbs with its French-style arches and vaulted ceilings, we were instantly smitten. For the owners, Kim and Karl, the flame was set on a slower burn, and our challenge was finding ways to fan it. The process ended up being an enlightening journey for all of us.

Far from being homebodies, this globe-trotting couple hadn't yet set foot in the apartment they had bought. They couldn't picture it as much more than a place to rest their heads between travels, and it was clear that their lifestyle wouldn't be centred around cooking and entertaining. Our usual process is to help people work out how to live in the home they love, but this time we were helping them love the home they were going to live in.

Our clients both liked the interiors style of Parisian apartments and wanted this place to exude the understated luxury of a favourite hotel room. That feeling of quietude and repose, of stepping into your own little world – and, of course, those indulgent elements, such as the plush carpet, the enveloping sofa and the high bed you almost need to climb into.

Luxury can mean many things, but for us it is found in a generosity of space, a sense of serenity and a richness of colour and materials that enhance your living experience. This apartment on the top floor of a Spanish mission-style building already boasted wonderful proportions and decorative elements. Our approach focused on reconfiguring areas to improve the flow and celebrating the romance and nostalgia of the property's heritage by bringing back the elegance of its spaces.

A significant step was turning one whole side of the U-shaped apartment into a master suite – an expansive carpeted zone that is all about restfulness. Repurposing a spare bedroom as a dressing room to remove a cumbersome wardrobe from the master bedroom was a strong contributing factor to the generous feeling here. It freed up the wall of the master bedroom, restoring the room's proportion and balance, and allowed the windows to reclaim their symmetry and the bed to be centred for a more pleasing aesthetic.

The size of the room meant we could embrace a little drama in the colour scheme. Marine navy walls augment the serene mood, and the burgundy and marigold linens of the custom bedhead offer a rich contrast and highlight its softly sculptural shape. The owners' vintage sideboard and bedside tables brought the warmth and solidity of timber, which we balanced with the rattan arcs of a mid-century armchair. The final component was a vintage leather screen, a decorative addition made possible by the newly empty wall. With an ornate vaulted ceiling, a view of the harbour and a heady blend of colours and textures, this space represents the ultimate in luxury.

On the other side of the apartment, we opened up the wall between the kitchen and television room by creating a huge archway with a sliding door. This offers a better connection between the spaces and allows the kitchen to benefit from the other room's harbour views. The kitchen's vaulted ceiling is uncluttered by cabinetry or recess lights. A discreet hanging strip light above the sink and a decorative pendant above the island are enough now that natural light also floods in. With cabinetry in a green so deep it is almost black, subtle brass accents and white glazed tiles, the kitchen is softly refined and welcoming.

Of all the spaces, the most luxurious in scale and nostalgic in ambience is the living area at the centre of the apartment. It is a gloriously bright room and its grand volume draws you in the moment you enter the apartment, an effect heightened by the original decorative arch at the end with another harbour vista. While solid French oak floorboards are laid straight throughout the apartment, their chevron pattern here is a response to the beautiful ceiling and a celebration of this special room.

The classic, formal nature of this space is balanced with a blend of contemporary, traditional and iconic pieces. We reproportioned a tiny fireplace to better align it with its tall mantel, adding a pink-toned marble hearth and flanking it with a pair of ebonised timber cabinets. The austerity of the pieces is tempered by the asymmetry of their height and the way they are dressed. Against the contrast of black and white, two velvet tub chairs bring a little romance with their delicate rose colour and stitching detail, and the lines of a mid-century table and chair further relax the setting.

The relationship between client and designer is a delightfully meandering one, and it was a joy to witness this couple's interest deepening during the process. We saw them come to enjoy the mix of elements – the way a vintage rug can bring an energy that is far from old-fashioned, and mismatched dining chairs can sit alongside a treasured family table. We shared in their growing appreciation of art, as they added their own discoveries to our suggestions. Their trust in us and their bravery in embracing this new home saw them sinking into their sumptuous new sofa, retreating to their bedroom sanctuary and even cooking in their elegant kitchen. This experience, of falling in love with something you didn't know you needed, is also one of discovering that your heart can be where your home is.

Far from being simply a decorative element, an artwork brings its own story and detail to an interior. The living room features three pieces of different media and styles that contribute to its lively mix. One of these, a figurative painting by Australian artist McLean Edwards, introduces another personality into the room, its captivating gaze wryly suggesting that the owners share the role of observed as well as observer.

THE PRESENCE OF ART

BELOW LEFT
Charlotte Perriand's ingenious Rio table for Cassina, which sits in the living area,
is one of several design classics that bring their own creative legacy to this interior.

BELOW RIGHT
In the master bedroom, the sculptural form of the bedhead with its burgundy and marigold
linens is a graceful decorative response to the romance of the apartment building's history.

OPPOSITE
The 19th-century embossed and handpainted Spanish leather screen makes a dynamic
grouping with the owner's vintage sideboard and the Sika-Design Paris chair by
Arne Jacobsen. The master bedroom's combination of warm tones and walls painted
in Dulux Hildegard is dynamic yet soothing in what is ultimately a retreat space.

LIGHT

WITHIN

'THE PALETTE OF EUCALYPTUS GREENS AND GREYS IS A CALMING REMINDER OF THE HOUSE'S CONNECTION TO ITS LANDSCAPE.'

# NATIVE HUES AND ILLUMINATION IN A CALIFORNIAN BUNGALOW

11 colours

310 m2

3 bedrooms
3 bathrooms
2 adults
2 children
1 dog
2 cats
1 cockatoo
1 lizard

Two sources of light wield a combined magic on the staircase of this lively family home. Above the sinuous line of a timber handrail that twists through the building's three storeys, an east-facing window offers a vast expanse of blue sky. Suspended before it, a large Akari light sculpture by Isamu Noguchi makes its delicate presence known and appears like a glowing sun or cool moon, depending on the time of day. It is a truly special moment – one of many in this house, where we used the opportunities offered by a particular space to embrace the transformative powers of light.

Opposite one of the best-known parks in Sydney's eastern suburbs, this three-bedroom Californian bungalow has undergone a modest renovation that is full of character and colour. Owners Merran and Aaron wanted an extension to the century-old house that could accommodate themselves, their two sons, two cats, a dog, a lizard and a cockatoo while still leaving ample garden and play space. Architect Ben Vitale created new open-plan kitchen, living and dining areas at the back, an upper storey that sits neatly behind the gabled roofline and a basement level, and we brought our vision for a harmonious meeting of old and new to the interior architecture and design.

The livability of a house is an ongoing focus for us, and as the kitchen is the centre of family life, we generally start our conversation here. Although a kitchen is a functional space, it needn't appear overtly so. We look for ways to make a kitchen feel more like a living area. The creation of a generous butler's pantry behind a series of doors was a significant factor in achieving that effect. A hardworking room packed with extra appliances, the pantry is still aesthetically pleasing, with glazed tiles, a glass-fronted cabinet and a little wooden shelf with an artwork sitting above. One set of doors conceals a welcoming bar area that is perfect for these regular entertainers.

With gatherings of family and friends in mind, we created a kitchen island with an open dining end that can accommodate six stools. The slenderness of the curved marble top, the slab of timber beneath, the timber legs and the fine bronze feet all emphasise the piece's lightness of form, giving it the style and convenience of a second dining table.

We were keen to use the light flowing through a small existing window on the wall behind the island, which features two rows of joinery handpainted in a deep green-grey. The luxury of the butler's pantry allowed us to relinquish some cupboard space in the upper joinery, so we reduced its length, allowing it to curve elegantly into the

wall beside the window. While the lower joinery extends further, the curved finish still allows plenty of room for the curtains to gather beside it. There is a sense that everything has room to breathe, and this effect is heightened by the floating linen curtains and two vast arched doors that connect this new space to the garden.

The generous flattened arch is repeated in a fireplace that we added in the new living area. This is a narrow space where smaller furniture makes a big impact through rich natural tones. In a room flooded with sunlight, a walnut bench and burnished brass coffee table glow on the vibrant patterned rug, enhanced by the forest green shades of the sofa and an artwork that is part of the couple's burgeoning collection.

Although the extension is contemporary, we were careful to honour the details of the original house. The arched doors and the grid moulding on the ceilings are a modern nod to the architraves and ornate ceilings in older rooms, while new tallowwood floors are laid in traditional block parquetry. A classical undertone connects the bathroom finishes: polished chrome, blackened bronze and the mosaic tiles of their curved walls – porcelain hexagons in deep sea green in the powder room, and tumbled marble squares in pale grey in the ensuite.

The palette of eucalyptus greens and greys is a calming reminder of the house's connection to its landscape. These beautiful tones intensify or soften as the light changes, with two spaces in particular – one old, one new – revealing their range.

The formal sitting room in the original part of the house was a dark, neglected area. To change the mood of the room and make it more inviting, we opened it up to the front garden and painted the walls a buttery green. A mix of chairs, a vibrant print, a burl coffee table, lightweight shelving and more curtains now contribute to create the welcoming, upbeat ambience that suits what is essentially a sunroom.

Upstairs, the neutral green on the wainscoted walls of the new master bedroom is a dreamy colour that alters according to the time of day and contrasts beautifully with the peach and rust tones of the bed linen. In this airy, inviting zone, there is a soothing sense of spaces talking to one another – outdoors to indoors, room to room. From the bedroom, you can see the sun's rays touch the grey cabinetry and the pink tones of the marble benchtop in the walk-in robe. From the top of the stairs, a serene corner of the bedroom beckons. Through billowing white curtains that pool gently on the floor, sunlight drenches a cosy lambswool armchair, creating another alluring moment in a house full of light and life.

Furnishings have much to say when it comes to enriching a colour scheme, as this vibrant living area reveals. Once the cool greens and greys of the built-ins were established, we brought in warmer tones as a lively counterbalance. The Fantaisie Impromptu rug by Halcyon Lake is central to that, with its collision of earthy colours. These tones are picked up in the timber De La Espada bench and aged brass Baxter table, as well as the Boffi Yak sofa with its tan leather shell. Green appears on the other Minotti sofa, but in emerald velvet that meets the richness of the scheme.

# LAYERING THE PALETTE

**ABOVE**
The dining space was designed in response to the living area and there is a lovely synergy
between the two through the interplay of tones. Around the Mads Johansen walnut table, the
tan leather seats and green frames of Gemla Vilda 3 dining chairs bring together the room's hues
of toasty terracotta and eucalyptus and olive green. An artwork by John Papas joins the curated
display of pieces along the wall.

**ABOVE**
The upstairs study is a robust yet comforting space layered with earthy colours.
Kvadrat woollen fabric in a russet tone adds a surprising soft element at the back
of the custom timber joinery.

**OPPOSITE**
The cool greens of the house shift to a buttery tone in the sunny sitting room, evoking an
entirely new mood. Here, walls painted in Dulux Sedia bring together the different pieces: the
defined lines of two Cassina Utrecht chairs and the curves of an Arne Jacobsen Charlottenborg
chair, the burl table we found in a Paris flea market and the artwork by Hannah Nowlan,
which hangs above the original marble fireplace.

TEA

THE

# AMONG

# TREES

'IT'S A PARTICULAR
QUALITY OF COLOUR:
YOU NEVER TIRE OF THE
HUES THAT TOUCH
YOUR EMOTIONS.'

# CREATING SPECIAL MOMENTS IN A FAMILY TERRACE

8 colours

295 m²

3 bedrooms
2 bathrooms
2 adults
2 children
1 cat

You can almost hear the birds chirruping and smell the fragrance of the flowers – such is the evocative power of the de Gournay wallpaper, which depicts a rainforest scene in an ombre wave of soft tones. This dreamy landscape completely transforms the long wall that connects the dining and kitchen areas of this home. It is captivating, immersive and one of those elements that we believe can be introduced purely for the pleasure it brings.

With some projects, we get the chance to evolve an interior over a period of time, enjoying an ongoing relationship with the owner. Our work on this three-bedroom terrace in Sydney's eastern suburbs spanned nine years and several incarnations. It began with a decorative scope and cosmetic changes, and moved to a redesign that incorporated new finishes and furnishings. What it proved was that some choices you make about colour, pattern and mood are resoundingly shown to be the right ones when you still love them many years later.

For Rachel and her family, the wallpaper is a firm favourite. Enhancing its appeal even further is the fact that rather than adorning a bedroom or other retreat zone, it appears in two utilitarian spaces, bringing its transportive charm to everyday activities. The wallpaper ties the narrow dining and kitchen spaces together and brings interest to both.

Of course, it doesn't work alone. The elegant simplicity of an Ilse Crawford timber bench and table complement the gradation of hues, and the thin slats of the bench's back allow glimpses of the rainforest. The bench hugs the walls, drawing the dining setting closer to maximise the available space. A coral-coloured rug and tan leather-seated chairs add warmth, and the final defining element is the matchstick bamboo blinds that cover an opening on the wall, pulling light in from a functional kids' zone while filtering the view of it.

When we returned to this house to redesign the kitchen, a focus for us was defying the narrowness of the space to create a grounded layout with a real presence, using a darker colour to bring depth. The stormy blue of the cabinets, with their classical detailing and gorgeously grippable brass handles, anchors the room and makes it appear more substantial. Most appliances are concealed, but a robust oven and cooktop, along with an aged zinc rangehood and grey basalt benchtops, heighten this effect. The kitchen becomes a strong punctuation in the rhythm of the house that invites you to stop and sit down. Even the white cabinetry that denotes the boundary of the kitchen encases function in beauty. The owner needed to put the laundry here, so we created storage that incorporates the machines but resembles a sideboard when closed.

A moody blue reappears upstairs in the deep slate of the master bedroom, where we experimented with deeper tones to calm and soothe. This was one of the first decorative choices in the house, and a testament to its success is that nine years later, after countless opportunities to update or change it, no one wanted to do so. It's a particular quality of colour: you never tire of the hues that touch your emotions.

That shade informed the scheme of the ensuite with its lighter grey-blue walls. There is a lovely, layered moment looking through the bedroom door where both blues can be seen. It gives a visual clue about how the two spaces work together.

In a challenging area, we addressed different floor levels with separate finishes, starting with grey terrazzo in the vestibule, then stepping up to elegant grey-white, blue and charcoal Moroccan concrete tiles in the ensuite. To increase the impression of space and sense of lightness, we designed a charming, freestanding armoire. Because this removed the need for under-bench storage, the delicate footprint of the sink barely touches the ground, keeping the focus on the patterned tiles that continue up the wall behind the vanity.

Patterned floor tiles bring another happy burst of colour in the family bathroom, in five combinations that range from sunny yellow to terracotta and sky blue to petrol blue. Balanced by blue wall panelling, white wall tiles and a grey marble bath and vanity, they lift the space and create a welcoming atmosphere.

In the front sitting room downstairs, several key pieces of furniture were part of our first decorative sweep, such as the coffee table, rug, sofa and armchairs. We designed the custom seating in shapes sympathetic to the era of the house. Their symmetrical layout is also quite traditional, but balancing elements, such as the contemporary table and textural sisal rug, relax the scheme. While the room has evolved with the addition of pieces like mid-century lamps and vibrant artworks, the original armchair upholstery we chose – a 1915 lotus-print fabric – remains another favourite. So too do the walls, painted in a shade enticingly titled Tea, which provides a beautifully warm, neutral backdrop to all the colour, pattern and art.

Years on from the start of the design process, it seems fitting that some of the boldest choices were the ones that still bring the most pleasure, from a rainforest-covered dining area to a room that speaks of tea and comfort.

The terrace typology of the long, narrow layout presented a challenge that we addressed through considered furniture choices. The dining area adjacent to the kitchen required a slim grouping of pieces that still allowed for a sense of flow. Aesthetically, the elegant form of the Ilse Crawford Low Settle bench for De La Espada seems to elongate the area, simplifying and calming the setting by reducing the amount of furniture. Functionally, it pulls the setting closer to the wall, while its high, slatted back protects the wallpaper behind. Anchoring the various pieces is the coral-toned Segovia rug by Robyn Cosgrove, which completes this cosy, inviting space.

# FURNISHING NARROW SPACES

# SEASON

'SPACES COME ALIVE
WHEN THE MATERIALITY
AND DECORATIVE ELEMENTS
MEET THAT OF THE
ARCHITECTURE.'

# CULTIVATING NEW ASPECTS
# IN A FEDERATION HOUSE

11 colours

270 m²

4 bedrooms
4 bathrooms
2 adults
1 dog

Sometimes the familiar patterns we have developed at home need a little shake up. Being shown a new way to experience our most loved spaces can be enlightening, offering even more possibilities of comfort and enjoyment. In this renovated Federation house in Sydney's inner west, it took some well-placed burl veneer and burgundy-hued marble to reveal those possibilities. The two materials became part of a rich tapestry of colour, texture and finish that transformed not only the house's interiors but also the perspective of its owners.

Following the visionary work of architects Welsh + Major, the owners, Karen and Bill, were living in a house that retained many attractive original features at the front and now had a light-filled extension at the rear and a contemporary garden pavilion. They sought our help to furnish their new living, dining and kitchen spaces in a way that would enhance their character and comfort, and create a more engaging experience for entertaining the extended family and guests who regularly come to stay.

In the way of many projects, our brief expanded the longer we spent with this sophisticated, open-minded couple who relished the process of seeing their home evolve with the introduction of contemporary, custom and vintage pieces and a more considered display of their art collection. Our attention to furnishings broadened to include built-ins, and the spaces we looked at extended to the front room, the master bedroom and the pavilion by Welsh + Major, which sits in a new garden designed by the late Peter Fudge. As the owners described how the trees change their hues throughout the seasons, it became clear how much they enjoyed interacting with this garden and its shifting palette.

With only floor-to-ceiling windows separating the garden from the living room, our furniture choices were about ensuring the view was uninterrupted. We replaced traditional rectilinear pieces with a single curvaceous sofa that gently draws your eye outside while echoing the lines of the owners' Swan chairs. The ivory of the sofa and the lilac shade of the chairs team beautifully with the coral-toned rug, each picking up the colours of the leaves outside. A small glass-topped coffee table and a cane chair complete an arrangement that is lightweight, open and relaxed.

Behind the living area, the owners loved sitting at their dining table to enjoy the garden vista, but we saw an opportunity to improve on this. Often the back wall of a room can provide a view into the buzz of activity, so we designed a built-in banquette, adding a table nook in burl veneer with a top of Rosso Levanto marble. It is

a perfect morning coffee spot and a natural place to congregate.

The burgundy marble and golden burl take their warmth from the timber dining setting, newly sanded floors and the terracotta tones of the artworks on the walls. They reflect the painterly approach we took to colour and texture in the house, reappearing in another setting we added to offer the owners a different way to use their space. The kitchen was full of stark white surfaces, so we refaced the joinery in limed oak, painted the walls a soft grey-green and created a new island base in burl veneer. They didn't want a dominant kitchen with the island as focal point, so we integrated a small cafe-style table with a marble top at the end of the island and added two bar stools to make it a lively spot for coffee, drinks and conversation. Family and guests now have a range of options from which to enjoy the entire open-plan space and the garden beyond.

While the placement of furniture can transform a room, colour also wields much power. With its rather cold palette, the neglected front sitting room wasn't the cosiest space, so we reset the tone by introducing a custom timber bureau in appealing hues of raspberry and coral that features intricate ribbon-style handles. It sparks a more vibrant mix of colours, and these continue in the vintage Chinese silk rug and eclectic accessories.

Spaces also come alive when the strength of the materiality and decorative elements meet that of the architecture. The rigorous details of the garden pavilion include a concrete and plywood ceiling and a timber inset in the concrete floor with a slatted edge that resembles the fringe of a rug. These inspired us to deliver a fresh interpretation of furnishings that reflect the owners' appreciation of not only design but also a melange of eras and styles. The linen curtains, in an ombre effect ending with a teal base, feature a wave motif in scarlet. This colour is echoed in a lacquer side table and the organic lines of the rug, and similar tones appear in the furniture and artworks.

Our textural journey continued in the master bedroom, where we refaced a white dresser with more burl veneer. The timber's warmth gently spreads to the existing bedside tables, which we sprayed a terracotta tone, and the bed with its turmeric-toned throw and linen. The bedhead in olive and ivory crewelwork offers another layer of colour and interest against the bottlebrush green walls.

The harmonious shifts between shades in this house work with its textures to accommodate family and friends in all its spaces. Like the changing palette of the garden, this is a place that adapts through the seasons to suit the lifestyle of its owners.

After witnessing how much joy these owners found in their glorious garden, we wanted to alter the perspective of the kitchen area by offering them another way to look out at the trees. In addition to modifying the existing island by layering different materials, such as a burl veneer, we added the small custom table with its brass base and Rosso Levanto marble top. By design, this reorients the owners' aspect, giving them a convivial new perching spot from which to enjoy their morning coffee and their garden view.

SHIFTING PERSPECTIVES

**ABOVE AND OPPOSITE**
Layers of colour in the master bedroom could have been distilled directly from the garden outside. The warm tones of the turmeric-coloured bedding join with those of the existing bedside tables, which we sprayed a terracotta colour, and the artwork by John Edwards. The olive crewelwork fabric by Pierre Frey draws intensity from walls painted in Dulux Tarzan Green, against which a Clam chair by Philip Arctander offers a light, frothy retreat spot.

# EARTH,

# AND

# SEA

SKY

'A DESIGN THAT
MERGES EARTHINESS
AND REFINEMENT,
FUNCTIONALITY
AND BEAUTY.'

# NATURAL TONES AND TEXTURES IN A COASTAL HOUSE

8 colours

320 m²

4 bedrooms
4 bathrooms
2 adults
3 children

It began with a new kitchen and a blue the shade of the ocean on a cloudy day, but the design for this house belongs to a bigger narrative that spans ten years. One of the most rewarding aspects of an ongoing relationship between designer and client is the mutual trust – your understanding of their likes and lifestyle, and their faith in your vision and aesthetic guidance. As that trust grows, we love opening our clients' eyes to new possibilities and seeing them challenge themselves with style choices they hadn't previously considered.

After working with the owners, Michele and Andrew, on three projects over the past decade, it was a pleasure to join them on their latest venture, a two-storey house near one of Sydney's best-known beaches. With their three children now grown, they are in a new phase of their lives, spending more time working, living and entertaining in this house that had originally been bought as a weekender. We had already done some small cosmetic work for them here, but now they wanted to feel it was truly their own place, not just one they visited.

On the crest of a hill between beach and bay, the house enjoys the distant blues of each view and is surrounded by towering gum trees. The language of the Australian landscape infuses the interior design, from the existing timber elements we retained to the earthy materials and colours we introduced, including that special blue in the kitchen. The granite benchtops and splashback, and the painted cabinets that reveal the grain of timber beneath their hue, are a world away from the ubiquitous blue and white palette of coastal interiors. This elegant smoky slate tone elevates and anchors the space, giving it solidity and character in an open-plan layout that also includes living and dining areas.

Offsetting those blue surfaces is a smooth cantilevered walnut slab that we added to the island. Not only does it establish a lovely connection to the owners' kitchen at home, which has a similar feature, it also merges practical and aesthetic considerations. The owners wanted a sink in the island, and the slab obscures the view of the sink from the entertaining side of the room without obstructing the line of cabinets underneath. As well as being a visual break, it creates an evocative area to gather around, offering the inimitable feel of timber for family and guests to lean on.

The attention to materiality continues on the stucco wall behind, which is painted a soft shade of parchment. Here, another slab of walnut is a shelf for objects, above a mirrored splashback that reflects the water beyond. The mirror appears to deconstruct the surfaces on the wall, creating an optical effect that sees the kitchen occupy indoors and outdoors at once.

Further back, from the living area, the blue planes and reflected glimpses of nature settle into the background. We used the same blue for the new joinery in the casual living room, a space made for lounging, games, watching television or just gazing into the fire. Arched doors with rattan panels slide open to reveal either the television or shelves, again integrating the practical and the aesthetic.

The existing sandstone fireplace, which is a chunky, dominant form, needed furniture that would contrast rather than add to its bulk. We replaced a heavy white sofa with a smaller, more tailored one and introduced furniture on legs to create a sense of lightness. A pair of slender leather armchairs in buttery tan, a petite coffee table and a drinks trolley deliver the sophisticated yet snug setting the couple wanted.

Beside this, the sitting room features a more traditional arrangement, with two sofas facing each other across a custom marble coffee table. The set-up is conducive to chatting and interaction, and the table is a generous platform for food and drinks. The spatial challenge that these back-to-back areas presented was that we had to ensure there wasn't too much furniture and that each space had a purpose. They each have to work in isolation but also together. One is geared towards entertaining, and the other towards intimacy, but both offer a seamless convivial experience when the house is full of people.

And both, like the kitchen and adjacent dining area, connect to the garden and trees that can be seen through the timber doors, frames and blinds. We were keen to keep these elements because they are so evocative of the Australian bush and tie the interior to the landscape.

If the downstairs rooms are defined by tree trunks, the ones upstairs are perched in the canopy. The high raked timber ceiling of the family room gives it a resort-like feel that, together with a beach-themed painting, led us to create relaxed seating that would have been out of place downstairs. This room also includes a study and television area that presents a distillation of greens from the walls to the cabinetry and marble benchtop.

Ten years ago, the owners may not have embraced the colour choices in this house. That confidence has developed from our long and evolving relationship with them. The same assurance is behind the hues and patterns of the different bedheads, from a teal botanical print in the master bedroom to a buttery graphic print and fringing in another bedroom. Those moments, amid a design that merges earthiness and refinement, functionality and beauty, are testament to a creative process built on trust.

ABOVE
The smoky slate blue of the kitchen continues in the joinery of the casual living room.
Here, furniture designed along small, slender lines contrasts with the solid form of the
existing sandstone fireplace.

OPPOSITE
A painting by Susan Rothwell creates a captivating trompe l'oeil effect in the family room
upstairs. Inspired by the artwork's transportive quality, we introduced a little laid-back coastal
style in the seating, which is balanced by the surrounding earthy palette.

In this special coastal home, we embraced colours that happily defy the typical beach aesthetic. A mix of different tones and textures in the bedrooms gives each its own distinct personality, with bedhead fabrics playing a vivid part. Here, the buttery hue of the Cosmico Ikat fabric by Clarence House on the bedhead is teamed with linen in a wash of pink and peach tones by Italian linen house Society Limonta. Far from the archetypal marine and white, they enhance the earthy, nuanced palette that distinguishes the house.

# DEFINING A NEW PALETTE

OF THE LA

THE

NGUAGE

HOME

'THE USE OF TIMBER CONTRIBUTES TO AN AUSTRALIAN VERNACULAR THAT IS PARTICULAR TO THIS HOUSE.'

# ENHANCING LOCAL CHARACTER IN A WATERFRONT HOUSE

10 colours

220 m²

4 bedrooms
4 bathrooms
2 adults
1 child

In a waterfront house, the view naturally takes centrestage, and people tend to gravitate towards it. This challenges and inspires us to ensure that the rest of the house offers an experience that is just as special. Sometimes this means bringing out the unique character of the less-frequented or overlooked spaces. In this two-storey house in one of Sydney's oldest inner-city suburbs, there's a little sunken room that is the furthest from the harbour frontage, but still draws people in with its warmth, wit and energy.

When we began work on this new house, the view wasn't the only factor to consider. There was also the building form itself, with its slanted roof and angled highlight windows, long skylight through the centre of the house, and concrete floor and plywood ceilings on the lower storey. There were the trees outside – a commanding gum tree and a jacaranda – which, together with the interior architecture, would lead us to embrace an Australian vernacular in the materials, colours and finishes. And then there were the owners, who wanted a 'barefoot house' with an easy, relaxed ambience for themselves and their young daughter.

Early on, they showed us a few of their existing pieces: some artworks, which represented just a part of their sizeable collection, a set of lovely, handcarved teak dining chairs and one very striking piece – the Up5_6 armchair and ottoman by Gaetano Pesce. With its playful curvaceous form swathed in bold red and white stripes, this is a design icon. The moment we saw the chair, we knew it would be the star of the sunken room and the starting point for a space full of character.

What began as an area without purpose is now a colourful library and happy hub for reading, games, watching television and just hanging out. Opposite the chair, an L-shaped leather sofa packed with cushions is designed for sprawling on, and a wall of metal-hung shelving holds a colourful array of books. On another wall hangs a collection of pages from old French wine catalogues, providing a vivid, fun display. With a stunning vintage light at each end and more lamps tucked into the shelves, the room has a welcoming glow.

The library's vibrant personality is balanced by the softer colours and robust materials of the quieter spaces near the harbour view. At the foot of the stairs sits the kitchen, where deeper tones and interesting textures enrich the space between the concrete floor and plywood ceiling. Smoked oak cabinets bring an earthiness to the classic forms of the cabinetry and the island bench with its dolomite top. There is a sense of calmness and timelessness here, with no full-height cabinets and nothing too utilitarian on show. Even a practical element like the stainless-steel benchtop features only the smallest upturn against the soft off-white wall. With a charming shelf for displaying objects, and terracotta red stools, the kitchen is just as much an appealing living area as a functional zone.

Opposite the kitchen are the living and dining areas, occupying a long yet compact space that stretches towards the water. Between these areas, we introduced a freestanding, double-sided gas fireplace with white glazed bricks that offer another appealing layer of texture. Without blocking the view, the low fireplace separates the two areas, allowing each to have its own distinct character. The dining area, with the family's teak chairs and a new timber table, is a warm, grounded setting beside the studio, while the living area features a pleasing medley of blue, green and grey that responds to the water beyond. Beautiful pieces of furniture hail from local and international designers, but something in their materials – the basket-weave chairs, the timber coffee table – channels a breezy holiday house vibe where time stands still.

The use of timber contributes to an Australian vernacular that is particular to this house. There is something almost reassuringly retro about the tallowwood used for all the doors and frames. It prompted us to explore a palette of eucalyptus greens and blues, inspired by the trees outside. The three upstairs bathrooms, with their mitred tallowwood mirror frames and cabinets in teal, blue and green, are variations on that palette. The flooring includes a pattern of three cheerful blue concrete tiles in one bathroom and vitrified porcelain tiles, in forest green and charcoal, in the others. Terrazzo features on the vanities of all three bathrooms, bringing a beautiful materiality and sense of nostalgia.

Two final spaces complete the rhythm of the house. The master bedroom, up in the treetops and enjoying a full view of the bobbing boats outside, appears almost unadorned. It has no curtain and just the softest of hues in the furnishings. In contrast, the powder room downstairs delivers a surprising punch of colour with walls painted deep russet red, a tone echoed in the terrazzo splashback. The powder room's palette began with a sandy hue, but when the rest of the design had been completed, we felt it needed more intensity.

Opportunities to elevate a space arise at every stage of the design process. Here, they began with a beautiful armchair that guided us in creating the design for the library and ended with a playful flourish that balances this home's more serene spaces. There are endless possibilities in a house where every space is special.

BELOW
At the centre of the timber dining setting, the clashing finishes of the Murano glass vase and terracotta bowl signal the alchemy of elements that create the magic in this home. Raw and honed, rough and polished play together in a design that celebrates the mix and meaning of its varied materials.

OPPOSITE
The freestanding fireplace delineates the living and dining areas, allowing each space to have its own character. The calm mix of blue, green and grey in the living room connects to the water beyond and includes the Walter Knoll Onsa chair and a sofa by Adam Goodrum beneath paintings by Joshua Yeldham.

Terrazzo introduces an earthiness of materiality that suits the relaxed mood of the house. We used slabs rather than tiles to give the smooth, seamless appearance of traditionally poured terrazzo. In this powder room, the colour of the materials elevates the space, with the vibrant reds of Signorino 987 terrazzo meeting the strong hue of Taubmans Really Russet on the walls. To mark the change in materials we used a little brass trim, which brings its own special finish.

BOLD MATERIALS

WALK

DERLAND

'THERE IS SOMETHING NOSTALGIC AND CALMING ABOUT THE COOL GREEN OF THE TERRAZZO TILES THAT BRINGS AN OTHER-WORLDLY MOOD TO THE SPACE.'

# CREATIVE WORLDS COLLIDE
# IN A FEDERATION HOUSE

7 colours

250 m²

4 bedrooms
2 bathrooms
2 adults
3 children
1 dog
1 cat

It was only a moment, but time seemed to stand still. We had just enjoyed a cup of tea in the kitchen with the owners and architect while we chatted about renovation plans, and before the light drizzle outside gained momentum, we all stepped into the garden. The conversation naturally turned to our surroundings – the 2400-square-metre garden had been a labour of love for the family for some years now – and standing amid the tapestry of colours and textures, we almost forgot why we were there.

Gardens do this, of course, evoking a sense of timelessness, wonder and utter tranquillity that transports you from the everyday. It was easy to see why this one, created by landscape designer Thomas Ellicott in Sydney's leafy north shore, had enchanted owners Margo and Ewan, and we in turn were romanced by their passion for it. Working with them and Margo's sister, architect Polly Harbison, to create a design that brought that sense and those colours and textures indoors became a labour of love for us too.

Much of our work involves collaboration, but there was something about this project, its joyous spirit and collective energy, that went far beyond that first cup of tea. This is a design that not only brings together the hearts and minds of the people involved, but also celebrates the synergy of building and garden, of architecture and materiality. The seeds had been sown on family holidays, when Polly sketched ideas for the extension to Margo's Federation house. Her concept for the architecture was a strong, almost brutalist structure of concrete, brick and timber that uses clever plays on scale to visually draw the garden and house closer. Our aim was to meet that strength with an intensity and depth of materials that enriched the living experience for the couple and their three daughters.

The feeling of being transported to another world is at its most powerful at the threshold between old house and new. A series of stepped spaces unfold towards the garden, their dimensions increasing beneath the one ceiling height as you move from the original house down to the new kitchen and outdoor courtyard, and down again to the living and dining areas, master bedroom and ensuite. The dramatic increase in scale, which feels a little like Alice's entry into Wonderland, culminates in the living area with its four-metre ceilings.

With everyone referring to it as 'the garden room', and the owners' request to feel as if they were living in the garden, our thoughts for this space turned to the dreamy indoor/outdoor worlds of loggias and Italian villas, which inspired the idea of a bordered and checkerboard green and white terrazzo floor. There is something nostalgic and calming about the cool green of the terrazzo tiles that brings an other-worldly mood to the space. To reflect the increasing scale of the architecture, we used the same tiles in a smaller format in the kitchen and larger ones in the garden room and master bedroom. Just as the garden appears to be creeping inside, the house seems to be growing out to meet it.

Materials and colour play a vital role in the way people live in their spaces. We knew that smooth, all-white walls would have been overpowering in such a large area, so we opted for a roughly rendered finish painted a soft grey-green. The slightly rustic, textural look and soft tone merge with the garden beyond, which is beautifully revealed by sliding timber screens.

With the decorative beauty of the garden and the checkerboard floor, very little was required in terms of furnishings to create a convivial, layered space. Sculptural vintage wicker chairs provide a filtered peek at the greenery, while a vintage screen and a plant in an oversized terracotta pot help to modulate the room's height. Like the seasonal plantings, these pieces can easily be moved and replaced, allowing the space to grow and evolve with the family's style. The tiles take on the role of a rug here and in the master bedroom, where a tapestry we found in a Paris flea market presents a garden scene on the wall that is almost like a trompe l'oeil. Opposite, the real thing looms and blooms large, and the garden almost becomes the final wall of the bedroom.

It's another dreamlike shift in scale that is continued in the adjacent ensuite, a small space accessed through an elongated archway. The room's size allowed for a vivid explosion of materiality, so we concocted a jewel-box palette of green marble for the vanity, high-gloss green drawers and tamarind-coloured walls, and the whole room is enveloped in the warm glow of teak. Richly layered and luxurious both in its aesthetic and its experience, this feels like no other space in the house. From here, the scale expands again to an outdoor shower that is all exposed bricks and open sky.

In the ensuite, the colours exude drama, but in the kitchen they bring balance and harmony. The interior story of green actually begins here, in the tranquil tones of the cabinetry, paired with teak to create a warm, inviting and livable space. At the centre of the house, this vibrant room connects spaces and people, enticing nature inside with its palette and bringing the family together in their own wonderland.

The enchanting connection between the house and garden –
the way each appears to be unfurling towards the other –
inspired this verdant palette. An evocative collision of greens
includes the deep hue of Dulux Nimrod on the kitchen joinery,
the misty haze of Dulux Water Rock on the walls, the intensity
of Dulux Briar on the high-gloss bathroom cabinets and the
rich, layered greens of the stones: Verde Esmeralda marble
in the bathroom and Verde Alpi in the terrazzo floors. These
beautiful tones entwine and diverge, establishing a magical
interior garden of their own.

# REIMAGINING GREEN

BELOW

With the kitchen to the left and courtyard to the right, the series of expanding volumes
in the house work with the alluring path of green to draw all towards the garden.

OPPOSITE

A little breakfast bar in the kitchen is a functional zone that allows the island to remain
a calm spot for people to gather. Together the green cabinets, the warmth of teak, the beautiful
veins of Arabescato Vagli marble and the texture of Moroccan glazed terracotta wall tiles all
contribute to the depth of materiality.

A WALK IN WONDERLAND

A richly layered explosion of materiality and colour, the master ensuite offers a unique experience in a house full of special moments. The vivid greens of the marble and cabinetry contrast with walls painted in Taubmans Jandakot and the teak surrounds. The white basin seems to hover like a crisp, clear pool in their midst.

With the abundance of the garden facing it, we kept the decorative scheme of the bedroom fairly pared back. The tiles act like a wonderfully bold rug, while the vintage tapestry, which we found in a Paris flea market, echoes the greenery before it.

AGEING
GRA

CEFULLY

'THE HOUSE NAVIGATES ITS OWN BEAUTIFUL BALANCE OF STREAMLINED ELEGANCE.'

# FUSING OLD AND NEW
# IN A 1930S VILLA

5 colours

460 m²

5 bedrooms
4 bathrooms
2 adults
4 children
2 cats

When it comes to incorporating a new design into an older building, one of the signs of a harmonious fit is a sense that the finished house has always looked this way. To elevate the original space, we consider where to add but also where to hold back, where to restore certain features and where to extend and even replicate them. We trod that delicate line in this elegant 1930s villa in Sydney's upper north shore.

With its gracefully curved exterior and its attractive interior staircase, the house retained elements of its original P&O architectural style, but after undergoing an extension in the 1980s it suffered from a disconnect between old and new. This was particularly evident in the building fabric of the interior, where areas in the extension felt less substantial than others in the house. There was also an awkward configuration of rooms, with the original kitchen tucked away in the back corner of the house, far from the living room on the opposite side. And finally, there was a lack of interaction between the house and its rambling front garden.

For the owners, Sophie and David, and their four daughters, the layout wasn't compatible with contemporary family life. Working closely with them and architect Luke Moloney, we set about replanning the three-storey house, particularly its first floor, where the main living areas are.

The first step was visually unifying the house through its palette. While the exterior was already white, different colours inside highlighted the uneven layout. We painted the interior walls white, the doors and window frames black and had the timber floors polished and stained with a Black Japan finish. The crisp, graphic contrast of black and white brings the disparate elements together and calms everything down. It also relates aesthetically to the era of the building and provides a neutral backdrop for the owners' changing display of artworks.

The contrast comes into its own in the new kitchen, which we relocated to the centre of the house, replacing a former living area. With a wall of soft grey cabinets and a black-stained oak island, the space is quite pared back in terms of its materiality, but details of line and finish add interest. The island itself is an almost monolithic piece that gives the room a real presence, but the intricacies of its design balance its form. Against the black timber, brass accents glimmer and shine, and the brass edge under the bull-nosed marble top echoes the brass lip on the base's curved plinth.

Fine timber frames around doors and drawers prevent the pale cabinets from appearing austere, and there is more brass in the custom-made arched handles. Brass ribbon-like handles feature on a tall black display cabinet opposite the island – a handsome piece with arched glass doors that also hides the everyday appliances sitting behind it. With those functional fixtures out of sight, and the understated simplicity of the classic white marble benchtop and splashback, there is a quiet strength to the kitchen. It is the heart of the house, sitting between the entrance on one side and the new living and dining areas on the other, and now offers a more connected experience.

To bring a similar sense of gravitas to the adjoining living area, we introduced a large fireplace to add some solid building fabric. There's something deliciously cosy about a fireplace and the way it gives a room purpose. People are drawn towards a hearth whether or not there is a fire burning. After removing a strangely situated fireplace from what is now the kitchen, we still felt that such a feature was important to the house's heritage. Carved from concrete block and rendered, the new fireplace is an attractive focal point that anchors the room, and it feels as if it has always been there.

At the other end of the extension, the dining area is centred around an inviting banquette in forest green leather, which offers a special outlook through the living area to the treetop aspect beyond. Green also makes an impact in the powder room, which features emerald and white tiles in a deconstructed geometric pattern across the floor and up to dado height. Softening the striking lines of the tiles is the pleasing single curve of an arched mirror – another link to the 1930s style.

A more significant new curve graces the exterior of the house, merging old and new and enhancing interaction with the garden below. In collaboration with Luke, we extended the space off the kitchen and introduced a balcony with a white rendered and framed wall that replicated the language of the existing entry portico. The addition of a brass rail above the balustrade to meet a height requirement is the finishing touch on this seamless architectural integration.

Inside the entrance, there is one last enticing curve. Its importance is defined by what we didn't do, rather than what we did. Up close, the shapely timber stair rail and balustrade reveals years of wear and tear and many layers of finishes. We left its treatment until the end of the renovation, but by then we had come to love how those marks of time and attention give it a warmth and character that simply couldn't be bettered. With existing elements like this, and the incorporation of new ones into the design, the house navigates its own beautiful balance of streamlined elegance.

Romanced by the existing architecture, we introduced finely crafted details that would complement and connect to the original design. We often talk about elements such as handles and lighting being the jewellery of the home. In this kitchen, both elements are slim in design, contributing to but not competing with the overall scheme. The brass and timber handles were custom designed to give a nod to P&O style, offering a contemporary interpretation that pays respect to the architecture. The brass strip light talks to the other brass elements, but with the island already making a statement, the light's role is more subtle and functional, casting a glow on the feature furniture piece.

FINISHING TOUCHES

Given the contrast of black and white in the house, we wanted a striking graphic effect in the powder room. The emerald and white tiles make an impact in this small space, with the single curve of the mirror offsetting their strong geometric lines.

In the kitchen, the fine timber frames of the joinery, the custom brass and timber handles, and the Carrara marble benchtop and splashback with its modest upturn all contribute to a look of understated elegance and classic simplicity.

# FAMILY

JEWEL

'WITH THE CURVES AND A MIX OF MATERIALS, THE KITCHEN IS A CLASSICAL ROOM WITH A FEMININE TWIST.'

# PRECIOUS PERSONAL SPACES IN A PARKSIDE TERRACE

**10 colours**

**230 m²**

**3 bedrooms**
**2 bathrooms**
**1 adult**
**1 dog**

Some designs are all the more rewarding for us because of their deeply personal nature, where creating something special for a client is an endeavour close to our hearts. This was the case the minute we met the owner of this 1890s Sydney terrace house and began crafting an elegant, inviting home for her that was full of wit and whimsy.

Maryanne had lived in this eastern suburbs house for a few years before she was ready to make it truly feel like her own place. A pleasant but tired-looking terrace facing the park, it had undergone an earlier extension that left behind an awkward floor plan and a lack of flow. Our design for the renovation focused on reconfiguring certain areas to bring in more light, a better sense of space, and a bespoke decorative approach that reflected her style and engaging personality.

If any space in this house illustrates the importance of understanding the owner's individual lifestyle, it is the new master bedroom. Rather than inhabiting the large front room on the first floor, which is usually chosen as the main bedroom in a terrace, our client preferred the quieter ambience of the back bedroom. It is a private spot with plenty of light and a pretty outlook over the back garden. This was a choice we quickly embraced when we appreciated the calm and sanctuary it brought her. The room itself, however, was poky and crowded. It had an ungainly ensuite, which we removed and rebuilt in the adjacent unused landing space. The new layout allows for a beautiful bedroom and sizeable ensuite without affecting the proportions of the other bedrooms or the second bathroom on this floor.

There is a pared-back delicacy to the master bedroom that evokes a wonderful sense of calmness and is attuned to a softly feminine quality. This is enhanced by the delectable vintage pink Murano glass wall sconces and some unexpected custom curves that we introduced throughout the house. On the ivory bouclé bedhead, the generous arch visually enlarges the room; on the linen curtains, the wave motif brings a serene sense of fluidity.

From this room, another series of curves can be seen in the ensuite, expressed in a vivid burst of pink. We started with a refined finish of milky grey marble floor and wall tiles, but, inspired by the owner's response to the design, we turned up the energy with a cabinet painted the colour of raspberry lipstick and an undulating Calacatta Viola marble benchtop. Above this, pink wallpaper with a repeated arch pattern continues the theme, creating a room that is dynamic, joyful and utterly appealing.

Downstairs, more whimsical waves appear in a relief pattern on the kitchen island cabinets and are echoed in the defined arch details of the French doors – a romantic element we introduced to connect this room to the internal courtyard. With the curves and a mix of materials that includes sage green cabinets, grey marble benchtops and brushed brass drawers, the kitchen is a classical room with a feminine twist. Some deft spatial manipulation, including the removal of a large column, allowed us to open the sink area to the courtyard and transform this narrow space into a light-filled room that appears larger than it actually is.

At one end of the island, we built a small banquette seat with a playful peach-toned ocelot print and had a piece of forest green marble made into a petite tabletop above a brass base. It is a sunny spot perfect for one – or two, with the addition of a chair – and it evokes a wonderful feeling of intimacy that extends from the kitchen to the casual living area on the other side. Light, welcoming tones feature in the furnishings here, and the space flows into the backyard through more French doors. Curves come courtesy of a television cabinet with a wave motif and a salmon-coloured sculptural table of reclaimed clay that has so much character you can almost picture it following the owner around the house on its robust legs.

As we designed these intimate spaces, we also had in mind the house's role as a hub for extended family. This is where the terrace's typical front formal living and dining rooms come into play, with the vintage dining table the scene of many gatherings. There is a lovely progression through these two spaces to reach the kitchen and courtyard, which is enriched by the connection of colours between the rooms and the hallway beyond. The butter yellow walls of both rooms create a warm, benevolent mood, against which the emerald dining chairs and the green and pink tones of the ottoman in the living room sing. These greens speak to the calming grey-green walls of the hallway, and the forest green ceiling in the entry offers another vivid moment.

A final joyful flourish in the second bathroom upstairs is as much a tribute to our client's enjoyment of colour as it is to her desire to incorporate spaces for visiting children and grandchildren. Positioned beside the other bedrooms, the room vibrates with hues, from the blue and orange Fornasetti wallpaper with its print of monkeys sitting in pomegranate tree branches, to the tiled floor with its pattern of colours spanning terracotta to ivory.

Our client's delight in every hue and every part of the process made it even more delightful for us to create a treasured personal space that is both a special home for her and the heart for her whole family.

ABOVE
The casual living area, which flows into the backyard through new French doors, is awash
with soft, light tones. A sculptural table of reclaimed clay by Ebony Heidenreich adds its own
wonderful character to the room.

OPPOSITE
Thanks to the pink Sandberg Marie wallpaper and the undulating lines of the custom vanity,
with its Calacatta Viola marble top and raspberry cabinet, the ensuite embraces the romantic
curves that feature throughout the house. These spirited, joyful elements were a response to the
owner's engaging personality.

We have a deep appreciation for the long heritage of craft and skill that wallpaper brings to an interior. The rigorous creative process continued by British wallpaper house Cole & Son has resulted in some of our favourite designs, including the whimsical prints of Italian icon Fornasetti. Their playful spirit is particularly appealing in intimate spaces, and the depth of line and colour in Frutto Proibito wallpaper, not to mention the surprise detail of its monkeys, enlivens this bathroom. Weaving humour into a design is a touchstone of our approach to so many spaces – a moment that elicits a smile can infuse the whole house with joy.

# WHIMSICAL WALLPAPER

# GREENE

## GREENE PAS

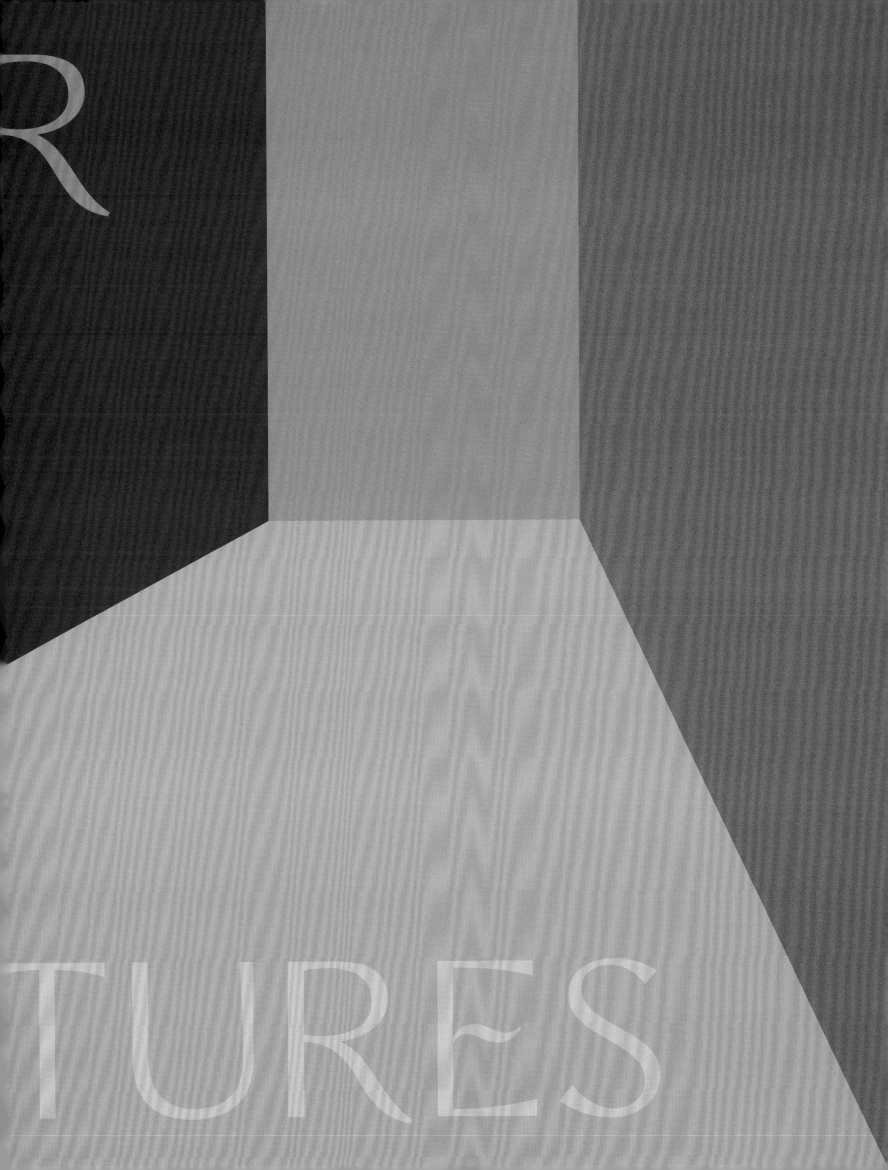

'THIS HOME APPEARS TO
BE INTIMATELY PART
OF THE LANDSCAPE.'

# CONNECTING WITH THE LAND IN A RURAL WEEKENDER

11 colours

620 m²

5 bedrooms
7 bathrooms
2 adults
3 children
2 dogs

Something magical happens during summer afternoons on this country New South Wales property. Outside, a languid stillness descends – with the exception of the surrounding garden, which hums with bees and butterflies – and the colours seem more intense. Inside the house, the rooms are bathed in sunlight that plays on the rich hues of the walls, the softer tones of the furniture and the warm timber and stone finishes. With the doors opening onto a deep wraparound verandah and every window offering its own special vista, this home appears to be intimately part of the landscape.

Rebecca and Graham sought that special connection to the land for this weekender they enjoy with their three sons. In the distance, the views of lake, grass and gum trees appear endless, while closer to home, work on the garden is progressing under the expert eye of landscape designer Paul Bangay. The building itself, mostly laid out over one extensive single storey, has the feeling of a sophisticated homestead, which we wanted to emphasise through an interior design that balances comfort and elegance.

Family and friends are always visiting and the place is often humming with lively gatherings. A range of living spaces was important, as was a hardworking kitchen. The only part of the house with a pitched ceiling, the kitchen evokes a country house ambience that we embraced by adding V-shaped grooved panels to the ceiling, and painting these and the exposed rafters white. Nods to tradition appear in elements such as glass-fronted upper cabinets and the timber legs and frame of the island, but these are all cast through a modern lens. The island's cabinets feature a contemporary interpretation of Shaker style and a simple slab of marble on top gives it a clean silhouette. We introduced strong natural colours to unify the space – the grey and caramel veins of the marble and the dark green of the cabinets that also appears in the terrazzo floor. The floor is another contemporary element that contrasts with the timber floors elsewhere and gives the room a robust feel.

Enhancing that feeling is a 'behind the scenes' area on the other side of the main kitchen space that features a fridge, pantry, breakfast bar and coffee station. Although concealed, it continues the room's beautiful details with glazed wall tiles in ivory and forest green, chic timber shelves and an old-school plate rack. This sleek functional zone allows a range of activities to take place while keeping the front of the kitchen a calm, effortless-looking space.

That sense of ease extends to the casual dining area in front of the island, where we included a bench in the timber setting to reduce the number of chairs and establish a more relaxed mood. This continues in an adjacent casual sitting area that has a built-in sofa bench and integrated table. Furnished in grey with soft pink tones, the sofa offers a quiet place for gazing at the lake.

This balance between comfort and elegance, country and contemporary, continues in the living and dining rooms, which are separated by a substantial stone fireplace. Light and airy, surrounded by tall windows and doors to the verandah, the living room features more traditional forms of furniture, and a ceiling grid augments its formality. The colours reflect the views outside – pistachio, forest greens and soft neutral tones offset the bold hues of a large contemporary artwork on one wall. The furnishings here are more about texture than pattern, and the layers of wool, linen and velvet come into their own in the colder months. When the doors are closed on winter afternoons, a sense of cosiness envelops the room, but it still maintains a connection to the changing patchwork of colours outside.

Just as the garden hums with energy, so too do the artworks, which bring a youthful spirit to the house. Another sizeable modern painting presides over the dining room, where the slim-lined timber setting keeps the space from seeming too formal. A slender pendant light allows an unobscured view of the brightly coloured work, and its leather and brass tie in beautifully with the house's aesthetic.

A very different landscape emerges in the generous master bedroom, where we introduced a scenic treatment on one wall to help reduce the scale of the room, which also features a lounge setting, fireplace and bath. The exotic rainforest-themed wallpaper sets the tone for this sumptuous space. With its walls painted midnight blue, a custom bedhead in scarlet velvet and bedding in luscious peach tones, this is an oasis of luxury.

In the ensuite, steely blue-grey cabinets continue that depth of colour beneath marble vanity tops of grey and terracotta. Those shades form a dynamic mix in the patterned floor tiles, and the milky glaze of wall tiles provides a soft foil for the outlook through the windows. Floor tiles offered us a lovely chance to play with the country motif in three other bathrooms. They create a fresh gingham-like pattern in colour groupings ranging from rose and terracotta to ivory, grey and black. Each complements the pastel hue of the room's vanity cabinet, while V-shaped grooved panelling delivers another casual homestead detail.

Every retreat space – vanity, bath, bed, sofa, even hallway nook – is linked to a view of the garden through doors, windows or reflections in a mirror. As the garden grows, the house will settle further into its landscape, the play of colours between inside and out will deepen, and the family can enjoy that special connection all year round.

**ABOVE**
The coffee station is one of the clever spaces behind the kitchen that enhance and extend its
functionality while allowing the room itself to remain uncluttered. Glazed forest green tiles
and cabinetry painted in Dulux Briar are an elegant pairing beneath an open plate rack,
which was requested by the owner and adds another country homestead detail.

In this hardworking house, a mud room was a natural addition and another of those practical areas we consider for families. This custom-designed drop zone for bags, hats, gumboots and raincoats features timber joinery with V-grooved panelling painted in two shades of blue – Taubmans Shindig and Saxby Blue. The warm tones of the upholstery are echoed in the leather handles and personalised leather and brass hooks. With a timber-topped island and drying cupboard, the room is a super-functional space made elegant by the intricacy of its details.

# ELEVATING THE EVERYDAY

LA EN

VIE

ROSE

'INSPIRED BY THE CHARACTER OF THE HOUSE AND THE ADVENTUROUS SPIRIT OF ITS OWNERS, OUR DESIGN FOCUSED ON STRONG SINGULAR GESTURES.'

# A MODERN VISION IN PINK FOR A VICTORIAN NEO-GOTHIC HOUSE

12 colours

240 m²

3 bedrooms
3 bathrooms
2 adults
2 children

You may not expect to come across an anthropomorphic wicker chair in the living room, feet planted firmly on a vintage rug, one arm permanently raised as if in greeting. But then neither would you expect a washed pink render and a brise-soleil of terracotta tiles, reminiscent of an Italian villa, on the exterior of a Victorian neo-Gothic house. What ties these features together is the lightness of spirit and strength of vision that characterise both the interiors and architecture of this home in Sydney's eastern suburbs.

When we were engaged to bring the drama of colour and materiality to this design, we worked in collaboration with architect Luigi Rosselli. Owners Sonya and Chris sought to improve on a recent extension to the rear of their 1880s house to bring in more light and establish a better connection to the expansive backyard. Rosselli's clever solution involved shaving off the extension, replacing it with an open-plan area for the living spaces on the ground floor and using the existing roof space to create an upstairs master suite and study. The beautiful brise-soleil, introduced to filter sun, adorns one wall of the master ensuite and runs along the roofline above the study.

There was a modesty to this project that appealed to us. No space is superfluous, and materiality and design take precedence over square metreage. The original part of the house at the front contains the two children's bedrooms, a bathroom and rumpus room, and the new extension houses the living, dining and kitchen areas in a compact space that doesn't *feel* compact. This is due to the generous volume created by the architecture, which features a series of sweeping curves, including a vaulted ceiling in the living area, a large arched window in the kitchen, a ribbon-like staircase and a dramatic arc in the rear wall.

Aligning our vision with Rosselli's, we responded to the sculptural elements of the architecture, the pink tones of the exterior palette and the spatial arrangement of the interior. Inspired by the character of the house and the adventurous spirit of its owners, our design approach focused on strong singular gestures, incorporating fewer pieces that are substantial in terms of design but still make this home eminently livable.

In the living area, the solitary modular sofa is upholstered in lilac chenille, an unexpected choice that is full of charisma and comfort. Sitting on a coral-toned vintage Chinese silk rug and flanked by two small tables, one vintage burl and one vivid green ceramic, the sofa is a voluminous piece, yet it doesn't dominate the room.

It was important to understand how spaces connected in this open-plan zone. With the dining area and kitchen running parallel to each other behind the sofa, we wanted to differentiate the form of the dining table from that of the island. The organic shape of the timber table takes on a dynamic asymmetry when viewed from various aspects in the house. The pale grey marble island, with its softening shark-nose top and fluting, anchors a kitchen rich in colour and texture. Offset by peach terrazzo floors, joinery painted a deep inky blue surrounds a splashback that ripples with hues from navy to grey to caramel. When sunlight floods through the large arched window, these tones and textures play happily together.

The strong colours of the marble, the shape of the dining table and the sofa upholstery all represent an unconventionality that began with the architecture and continues in the interiors. For the walk-in robe upstairs, we chose inset panels of wallpaper in an abstract landscape design by Faye Toogood that appears almost like an artwork in itself.

With its view of the greenery of the sloping garden by landscape designers Dangar Barin Smith, the adjacent master bedroom has a charmingly casual air. Across the golden ochre of the vintage rug, furniture is an eclectic mix of pieces that include a traditional Sri Lankan dresser, a trolley used as a bedside table, a vintage paper lantern and a little chair where Chris and the children play the guitars from his collection. In keeping with the house's layout of purposeful spaces, this is not a cocooned sanctuary but rather another living area perfectly suited to the family's lifestyle.

Playful decorative elements appear in the pink curtains with their mushroom fringing, in the fabrics Sonya found for the pillowslips and in the Japanese silk we used for a bolster. This owner's love of the handcrafted enjoys another moment in the rumpus room downstairs, where artworks, needlepoint and an assortment of quirky objects create a vivid display against the terracotta-coloured wall and the ecru curtains with their tobacco-toned base.

That respect for craft pervades the house, extending to its layered materiality. There is a mesmerising quality to the finishes in the master ensuite, with its grey travertine floor and benchtop, and the shimmering shades of its Moroccan glazed terracotta wall tiles. Through the filtered light of Rosselli's brise-soleil, the tiles transmute from cool grey to glowing pink, as if in close communication with the rendered exterior. They are complemented by the warmth of European beech vanities, which have a fine framing that we repeated in joinery throughout the house. In the bathrooms, the natural timber brings an earthiness; in the kitchen, its intricate grain is revealed beneath the inky blue stain.

The depth of colour in the kitchen ties the open-plan spaces together and is more than a match for the unique form of the human-like Nalgona Chair by designer Chris Wolston. In a project involving many bold decisions, this was a tribute to the owners' sense of fun and willingness to embrace a design that is full of verve and vision.

ABOVE
In the walk-in robe, panels of Faye Toogood's Woodlands wallpaper create a remarkable
painterly effect above the vibrant tones of a vintage rug.

OPPOSITE
Bathed in light from the brise-soleil, the beautiful mix of materials and colours makes the
ensuite a special place. The shimmering grey of the Moroccan glazed terracotta wall tiles
meets the warmth of the vanity's travertine top and beech cabinets, with the Murano sconce
providing a confection of icy pink above.

The enduring appeal of art and objects in an interior resides in how they reflect their owner's personality. The rumpus room features an eclectic collection and we wanted to create a space that was lighthearted yet meaningful and full of warmth to house these treasured pieces. Small timber shelves from Great Dane provide an opportunity for a couple of quirky arrangements on walls painted in Dulux Motueka. The terracotta hue of the walls works with the base of the linen curtains and contrasts with the steely blue Jardan sofa, forming a vibrant background to the pleasingly personal display.

# MAKING ROOM
# FOR PERSONALITY

# ACKNOWLEDGEMENTS

To Paulina de Laveaux and Evi O for their spirit and enthusiasm working with us both on this project, an endeavour much bigger and more fulfilling than we could have ever anticipated. Thank you also to Lisa Schuurman, Lorna Hendry and the team at Thames & Hudson. It has been a pleasure working with you all.

To Fiona Daniels for crafting so eloquently the stories around each of the eighteen homes in this book. Your support and dedication has been unwavering, and we will always be very grateful to you. Thank you also to Karen McCartney for introducing us.

To our team at Arent & Pyke, past and present, for their unique and exuberant creativity, passion and dedication. The friendships and relationships forged over the years are as special to us as the projects we have all worked on together over the past fifteen years. A heartfelt thank you to Genevieve Hromas whose creative genius and infectious spirit is evident in so many of the homes featured in this book. Thank you also to Lauren Black for boldly and courageously steering the A&P ship. A special thank you also to Thea, Alyse, Brooke, Roisin, Kerri, Angie, Giorgi, Kristen, Julia and Dominique, Shannon and Phoebe.

To our photographer Anson Smart, who has been elegantly and evocatively capturing our work for fifteen years – thank you for your friendship, humour and commitment. The energy (and tunes) on set makes working with you and Russell Horton an absolute joy. To our dear friends Steve Cordony, Claire Delmar and Megan Morton – the styling powerhouses of Australia and beyond – thank you for sharing your magic with us. Thank you also to Felix Forest, Prue Ruscoe and Olga Lewis.

To our clients for trusting us with their homes, and for allowing us to enter their worlds on such a personal level. Our work is equally an expression of all of the unique personalities that we meet via the work that we do.

To our incredibly talented and growing team of creative partners and collaborators. All of the makers, upholsterers, builders, joiners and specialist trades that we partner with in crafting the homes like those in this book. A special mention to Eddie Chedra, Morgan Ferry, Danny Aron, Edwin Odermaat, Inge Holst and Gary Galego, some of whom we have had on speed dial for the duration of the fifteen years of Arent & Pyke.

To our families, for their love and support, this book is a celebration of the love, joy and colour you bring to our lives.

To Franklin, John, Michael, Rosemary, Joy, Shontae, Marcus, Paul, Ben and Maxine (Sarah-Jane). To Matthew, Valentina, Paloma, Christine, Peter, Katrina, Francine, Mary, Frank and the Arent and Squadrito families (Juliette).

# ABOUT ARENT & PYKE

Juliette Arent and Sarah-Jane Pyke share a passion for design that places people at its heart. Their approach is deeply empathic and collaborative as they craft mindful interiors that respond to and reflect the lifestyles of their owners. For them, the beauty of design extends far beyond the decorative to wield a power that can transform lives, uplift the spirit and nurture the soul.

With combined backgrounds in architecture, interior design and fine arts, the pair brought their years of design expertise, rigorous attention to detail and visionary flair to form Arent & Pyke in 2007. Since then, the studio has built up a significant interior architecture and design portfolio that focuses on the human experience of design by forging strong emotional connections and eliciting joy.

Acclaimed by peers and press as exuberant, refined, authentic and exciting, Arent & Pyke's work has featured in numerous publications and won multiple awards both locally and internationally. In 2021, they were named Interior Designers of the Year at the Belle Fanuli Interior Design Awards, also winning Best Residential Interior. In 2018, they were one of six practices selected to exhibit in the National Gallery of Victoria's Rigg Design Prize and in 2019 they received recognition as the only Australasian practice in the prestigious AD100 France listing.

# PROJECT CREDITS

## SCULPTURE BY THE SEA

Interior designers: Sarah-Jane Pyke,
Juliette Arent, Genevieve Hromas
Builder: Oakland Design & Construction
Photographer: Anson Smart
Editorial stylist: Juliette Arent

## UNDER THE TREE

Interior designers: Sarah-Jane Pyke,
Juliette Arent, Dominique Brammah
Architect: Welsh + Major
Landscape architect: Sue Barnsley Design
Builder: SFN Build
Photographer: Anson Smart
Editorial stylist: Claire Delmar

## THE PATH OF COLOUR

Interior designers: Sarah-Jane Pyke,
Juliette Arent, Alyse Hyman
Builder: Dewcape
Photographer: Anson Smart
Editorial stylist: Claire Delmar

## A FRAME FOR LIVING

Interior designers: Sarah-Jane Pyke,
Juliette Arent, Genevieve Hromas, Alyse Hyman
Architect: Carter Williamson
Landscape designer: Hugh Burnett
Builder: Artechne
Photographer: Anson Smart
Editorial stylist: Olga Lewis

## RHAPSODY IN BLUE

Interior designers: Sarah-Jane Pyke,
Juliette Arent, Diana Ribarevski
Architect: Tom Ferguson
Builder: Steele & Associates
Photographer: Anson Smart
Editorial stylist: Megan Morton

## BROAD SPECTRUM

Interior designers: Sarah-Jane Pyke,
Juliette Arent, Thea Kiel, Brooke Perry
Architect: Sam Crawford Architects
Landscape designer: Dangar Barin Smith
Builder: Cumberland Building
Photographer: Anson Smart
Editorial stylist: Claire Delmar

## SEA CHANGE

Interior designers: Sarah-Jane Pyke,
Juliette Arent, Genevieve Hromas, Alyse Hyman
Architect: David Boyle
Landscape designer: Pangkarra Garden Design
Builder: Trademark Building
Photographer: Anson Smart
Editorial stylist: Claire Delmar

## TRUE ROMANCE

Interior designers: Sarah-Jane Pyke,
Juliette Arent, Genevieve Hromas, Shannon Shlom
Builder: Daran Building
Photographer: Anson Smart
Editorial stylist: Claire Delmar

## THE LIGHT WITHIN

Interior designers: Sarah-Jane Pyke,
Juliette Arent, Thea Kiel
Architect: Vitale Design
Builder: Ray Follett Prestige Building and Carpentry
Photographer: Anson Smart
Editorial stylist: Claire Delmar

## TEA AMONG THE TREES

Interior designers: Sarah-Jane Pyke,
Juliette Arent, Dominique Brammah
Builder: Cumberland Building
Photographer: Felix Forest
Editorial stylist: Claire Delmar

## IN SEASON

Interior designers: Sarah-Jane Pyke,
Juliette Arent, Genevieve Hromas, Thea Kiel
Architect: Welsh + Major
Landscape designer: Peter Fudge
Photographer: Anson Smart
Editorial stylist: Steve Cordony

## EARTH, SEA AND SKY

Interior designers: Sarah-Jane Pyke,
Juliette Arent, Thea Kiel
Architect: Susan Rothwell
Builder: Wrightson & Co
Photographer: Anson Smart
Editorial stylist: Olga Lewis

## THE LANGUAGE OF HOME

Interior designers: Sarah-Jane Pyke,
Juliette Arent, Sarah Johnson
Architect: Thodey Design
Builder: Albatross Constructions
Photographer: Anson Smart
Editorial stylist: Steve Cordony

## A WALK IN WONDERLAND

Interior designers: Sarah-Jane Pyke,
Juliette Arent, Genevieve Hromas
Architect: Polly Harbison Design
Landscape designer: Thomas Ellicott
Builder: Zandt Building
Photographer: Anson Smart
Editorial stylist: Steve Cordony

## AGEING GRACEFULLY

Interior designers: Sarah-Jane Pyke,
Juliette Arent, Dominique Brammah
Architect: Luke Moloney Architecture
Builder: Cumberland Building
Photographer: Felix Forest
Editorial stylist: Claire Delmar

## FAMILY JEWEL

Interior designers: Sarah-Jane Pyke,
Juliette Arent, Alyse Hyman
Landscape designer: Secret Gardens
Builder: Oakland Design & Construction
Photographer: Anson Smart
Editorial stylist: Claire Delmar

## GREENER PASTURES

Interior designers: Sarah-Jane Pyke,
Juliette Arent, Brooke Perry, Phoebe Stone
Architect: Strongbuild
Landscape designer: Paul Bangay
Builder: Pinczi Builders
Photographer: Anson Smart
Editorial stylist: Claire Delmar

## LA VIE EN ROSE

Interior designers: Sarah-Jane Pyke,
Juliette Arent, Genevieve Hromas
Architect: Luigi Rosselli Architects
Landscape designer: Dangar Barin Smith
Builder: Buildability Constructions
Photographer: Prue Ruscoe
Editorial stylist: Juliette Arent

# ARTWORK CREDITS

**SCULPTURE BY THE SEA**

| P. 21 | Ray Crooke |
| P. 24 | McLean Edwards |
| P. 28 | Garry Shead (left), David Band (right) |
| P. 29 | Ray Crooke |

**UNDER THE TREE**

| P. 33 | Leah Fraser |
| P. 35 | Judith Wright |
| P. 39 | Judith Wright |
| P. 40 | Christian Thompson AO |
| P. 43 | Freciano Ndala |

**THE PATH OF COLOUR**

| P. 47 | Michael McIntyre |
| P. 50 | Tim Summerton |
| P. 57 | Marisa Purcell (top left), Brendan Huntley (bottom left) |

**A FRAME FOR LIVING**

| P. 64 | Amanda Williams |
| P. 65 | Seth Diego Birchall |
| P. 67 | Seth Diego Birchall |
| P. 68 | Patrick Hartigan (left) |
| P. 69 | Seth Diego Birchall |
| P. 75 | Seth Diego Birchall |

**RHAPSODY IN BLUE**

| P. 79 | Philip Drummond |
| P. 81 | Masks from Sepik River in Papua New Guinea |
| P. 82 | Bui Huu Hung (left) |
| P. 83 | Tongan Barkcloth Ceremonial Tapa |
| P. 85 | John Gould |

**BROAD SPECTRUM**

| P. 89 | Wu Hao |
| P. 91 | Ildiko Kovacs |
| P. 92–3 | Alec Cumming |
| P. 97 | Ildiko Kovacs |
| P. 101 | Jin Jiangbo |
| P. 102 | Wu Hao |

**SEA CHANGE**

| P. 109 | Mitch Cairns |
| P. 113 | Mitch Cairns |
| P. 115 | John Reid (bottom right) |
| P. 116 | John Reid (left), Nyapanyapa Yunupingu (right) |
| P. 117 | Anna-Wili Highfield (sculpture) |
| P. 118 | Antonia Perricone |

**TRUE ROMANCE**

| P. 125 | Robyn Beeche (left), Cameron Stead (right) |
| P. 129 | McLean Edwards (painting), vintage from ALM Sydney (sculpture) |
| P. 130 | Cameron Stead (left), Vanessa Stockard (right) |

**THE LIGHT WITHIN**

| P. 139 | Laura Jones (painting), Odette Ireland (mobile sculpture) |
| P. 145 | John Papas (left), Julian Meagher (right) |
| P. 146 | Utopia Art Sydney |
| P. 147 | Hannah Nowlan |
| P. 148 | Mark Tweedie |

**TEA AMONG THE TREES**

| P. 153 | Jason Moad (left), Frank Hodgkinson (reflected), Jo Davenport (middle), John Olsen (right) |
| P. 156 | Yun Wei |
| P. 157 | Jo Davenport (left), John Olsen (right) |
| P. 158 | Clara Adolphs |
| P. 159 | Robert Henry Dickerson AO |

**IN SEASON**

| P. 165 | Janice Murray |
| P. 168 | Noŋgirrŋa Marawili (left), Elisabeth Cummings (right) |
| P. 171 | Bruce Goold |
| P. 173 | Elisabeth Cummings (refected) |
| P. 174 | John Edwards |
| P. 176 | John Bokor (bottom right) |
| P. 177 | John Bokor (top right) |

**EARTH, SEA AND SKY**

| P. 188 | Susan Rothwell |
| P. 189 | Susan Rothwell |
| P. 192 | Vintage artwork from Rudi Rocket (top right), artwork from Orient House (bottom right) |
| P. 193 | Susan Rothwell (top right) |

**THE LANGUAGE OF HOME**

| P. 197 | Eric Rimmington |
| P. 199 | Framed wine catalogues from 1930s |
| P. 200–1 | Tsuruya Kokei (left), Eric Rimmington (middle), Hideaki Yamanobe (right) |
| P. 202 | Framed wine catalogues from 1930s |
| P. 203 | David Welch |
| P. 204–5 | Joshua Yeldham (both) |
| P. 206 | Joshua Yeldham (both) |
| P. 207 | Nicholas Blowers (both) |
| P. 210 | Emma Walker (top right), Laura Jones (bottom left) |

**A WALK IN WONDERLAND**

| P. 223 | Margo Harbison |
| P. 224–5 | Artwork borrowed from vintage store |
| P. 226 | Vintage tapestry sourced from Les Puces de Saint-Ouen |
| P. 228 | Christina Cordero |

**AGEING GRACEFULLY**

| P. 239 | Faith Mrljak |
| P. 241 | Antonia Mrljak |
| P. 243 | Faith Mrljak |

**FAMILY JEWEL**

| P. 249 | Framed vintage textile |
| P. 251 | Framed vintage matchboxes |

**GREENER PASTURES**

| P. 267 | Lucy Culliton |
| P. 268 | Evanie Saunders |
| P. 272 | Ben Quilty |
| P. 273 | Ben Quilty |
| P. 274 | Guido Maestri |
| P. 277 | Simonn Schumacher |

**LA VIE EN ROSE**

| P. 297 | Clockwise from top left: needlepoint from Etsy, Bardayal 'Lofty' Nadjamerrek, Laura Skeri, Andy Harwood |

First published in Australia in 2022
by Thames & Hudson Australia Pty Ltd
Wurundjeri Country, 132A Gwynne Street
Cremorne, Victoria 3121
ABN: 72 004 751 964

First published in the United Kingdom in 2023
By Thames & Hudson Ltd
181a High Holborn
London WC1V 7QX

First published in the United States of America in 2024
By Thames & Hudson Inc.
500 Fifth Avenue
New York, New York 10110

Arent & Pyke and Thames & Hudson Australia wishes to acknowledge that Aboriginal
and Torres Strait Islander people are the first storytellers of this nation and the
traditional custodians of the land on which we live and work. We acknowledge their
continuing culture and pay respect to Elders past, present and future.

A catalogue record for this
book is available from the
National Library of Australia

ISBN 978-1-760-76249-0
ISBN 978-1-760-76317-6 (special edition)
ISBN 978-1-760-763954 (US edition)

British Library Cataloguing-in-Publication Data
A catalogue record for this book is available from the British Library

Every effort has been made to trace accurate ownership of copyrighted text
and visual materials used in this book. Errors or omissions will be corrected
in subsequent editions, provided notification is sent to the publisher.

Front cover image: Anson Smart
Authors' image on p. 301: Hugh Stewart

Design: Evi O. Studio | Evi O
Design Assistant: Evi O. Studio | Emi Chiba
Writing: Fiona Daniels
Editing: Lorna Hendry

Printed and bound in China by C&C Offset Printing Co., Ltd

Be the first to know about our new releases,
exclusive content and author events by visiting
thamesandhudson.com.au
thamesandhudson.com
thamesandhudsonusa.com